The Weapons · of Our

Warfare

Volume III

The Keys to the Kingdom

Confessing the Word of God with Authority

By Kenneth Scott

Scriptures in this publication are taken from the King James version of the Bible and paraphrased by the author.

The Weapons of Our Warfare Volume III
(The Keys to the Kingdom)
1st Printing

ISBN: 0-9667009-6-1

Copyright © 2002 by Kenneth Scott
Spiritual Warfare Ministries, Inc.
P.O. Box 2024
Birmingham, AL 35201-2024
(205) 853-9509

Contents

Contents Continued

Section III — Confessions

Dedication:

As with the other books in the sequel of the Weapons of Our Warfare, this book is also dedicated to my father in the faith, Bishop Nathaniel Holcomb. His anointed teaching and leadership inspired and helped to give me a good foundation, and also helped to establish me as a minister of the Gospel.

Introduction

The Greek definition for the word *confession* is the word, "*homologeo.*" This word has several definitions, which help us to better understand confessions. They are as follows:

1. "To <u>speak the same thing</u>"
2. "To come in <u>agreement</u> with"
3. "To <u>unify</u> with"
4. "To <u>declare</u>"

The first definition of confession is, "**to speak the same thing.**" What we speak is the Word of God. We are to speak the same thing that God has spoken in His Word. If there is a need in our lives, we are not to speak or confess what we think or feel about the situation, but rather find what God's Word says concerning our need, and then speak and say the same thing God's Word says about that need.

Agreement is, "**to be of the same opinion and mind.**" God's Word is truth. It is powerful, unstoppable, and awesome by itself. And, when we begin to confess the Word of God, our minds and hearts will line up with the Word of God (in faith), causing our situations and circumstances to also line up with the Word of God that we have spoken.

Unity is "**to come together and become united with one cause or purpose.**" It is also the place of consistent agreement. Confession is not something we should do every now and then, or when we feel like it, it's something we are to do consistently. If we are going to be developed in a life of confessions, we must become disciplined and consistent in praying and speaking the Word of God. When we do so, our lives and circumstances will also become united with, and line up with the Word of God.

To declare is "**to proclaim, pronounce, or make a declaration**." When we effectively make our confessions, we are (as kings), decreeing and declaring God's Word with His authority and power. And, as the words of a king must come to pass, our words as kings (unto Jesus Christ—the Most High King) shall also come to pass.

So with this understanding, confession is this: To speak the same thing God has spoken in His Word, causing us to be of one mind and opinion with His Word. This brings our situations and circumstances in line and in accord with God's Word, which brings us into unity, discipline, and consistency of the Word, enabling us to boldly decree and declare His Word with power and authority.

This is just a brief definition and explanation of confession. Section one goes into more details and explanation about confessions, what they are, and how they affect our lives and circumstances.

Section I

Understanding Confessions

Speaking Death or Life

Proverbs 18:21 Death and life are in the power of the tongue: and they that love it shall eat the fruit thereof.

We can either speak death and destruction to our lives by speaking negative words and confessions of doubt, fear, and unbelief, or we can speak the abundant life of God through speaking what God says about our lives.

In the beginning, when God created man (Adam), the Bible says that He breathed in Adam the *"Breath of Life*, and man became *"a living soul."* This phrase *"Breath of life,"* actually means, "the life, power, and authority of God." And, when it says that man became "a living soul," this actually means, **"a speaking spirit."**

God creates, changes things, rules, and reigns with His Word. And just as God creates, changes things, and rules with His Word, He has also created man as a "speaking spirit" to do the same. Even though God created all the animals, He only created man in His likeness and image. It was also only in man that God breathed *"the breath of life*,*"* which is **"the life of God."** And as a result of this divine impartation, man became "a living soul" (another "speaking spirit" like God).

John 1:12 But as many as received him, to them gave he power to become the sons of God, even to them that believe on his name:

Romans 8:14 For as many as are led by the Spirit of God, they are the sons of God.

The image of God represents this son-ship as seen in both passages above. If you are a believer, and you have been born again of the spirit of God, then you are one of the sons of God to whom these passages are referring. This phrase "sons of God" refers to both genders. Sons have the image and likeness as their father. God has created us in His image and likeness to be a "speaking spirit," to speak to our circumstances just as God speaks.

** For more information about the authoritive power that God has given to us as speaking spirits, please see our book entitled, "**Praying in Your Divine Authority.**"*

There are two diametrically opposed forces waiting for us to speak so they can bring actions to our words (angels and demons). Psalms 103:20 tell us that *angels hearken to the voice of God.* The voice of God is His Word. God has given us (as born-again believers) His authority to decree and declare His Word. When we speak the Word of God, angels move out on our behalf to bring God's Word to pass in our lives, and in the lives of others for whom we pray.

Satan and demon spirits also understand the authority and power of our words. And just as the angels of God move out to bring to pass the positive words (Word of God) that we speak, demons and devils also have the authority to move out and bring to pass the negative words that we speak. When we speak negative words and confessions, and words of doubt, fear, and unbelief, we are (with the authority of our words) giving them permission to use our own words against us, and manifest killing, stealing, and destruction in our lives and circumstances.

It's somewhat like the Miranda rights which are read to a person when they are placed under arrest. The arresting officer begins by telling the accused that they have the right to remain silent (if they choose so). The officer continues by telling the accused that anything they say can and will be used against them in a court of law. What they mean by this is that the prosecutor can take any confessions or words they speak and use them against the person in a court of law to prosecute and convict them.

Satan and demon spirits are our spiritual prosecutors. In Revelations 12:10, the Bible calls Satan, *"the accuser of the brethren."* In our modern-day terminology this simply means that he is a spiritual prosecutor. Satan and demon spirits are constantly lurking about us, listening to every word we say. They are listening to see if we will speak words of doubt, fear, and unbelief so that they can use them against us. When we speak them, we give Satan and evil spirits permission to use them against us and manifest them in our lives.

So again, we can either speak life to our circumstances by confessing the Word of God, and thereby allowing the angels of God to act on our words, or we can speak death, by either being negligent and failing to speak the Word of God, or by speaking words of doubt, fear, and unbelief (giving devils and demons permission and authority to use our words against us).

Rehearsing Your Script

When we confess God's Word, we are confessing the Holy Scriptures (the written Word of God). The root word of the word "scripture" is "*script*." A script is a prearranged written dialog or story line. First, a writer writes a story. Then, he assigns characters to his story, and assigns each character to a particular part or script. The actors must then take time to study their lines until they are learned. Then, at the appropriate time of action, they profess (or act out) words and actions according to their script. When it is all put into action, the actors bring life to a story that came from words written on a piece of paper (his or her script).

Spiritually speaking, God is the great author (*the author and finisher of our faith—Hebrews 12:2*). He has written, "*The greatest story ever told.*" The Bible is His story. Whatever we need in our lives is our script that we rehearse. As we continually rehearse or confess our script, we bring life to our situations and circumstances through God's divine authority and the power of His Word.

Again, whatever you need or desire for your life is your script. If you are believing God for healing, then you rehearse God's scripts concerning your healing. If you need finances, then you rehearse your script concerning your financial blessings. If you desire God's blessings in a particular area, find the scripts that pertain to that particular blessing and begin to rehearse them. And as you do so, like an actor brings life to a story from words written on a piece of paper, you will (through the power and authority of God's Word) bring life (manifested changes) to your situations and circumstances.

The Process of Prayer and Confession

Many people mistakenly believe that when they pray, if they have not received the answer to their prayers (in an assumed amount of time) that God has not answered their prayers yet. This is what the devil wants us to believe. The fact is, when we pray according to the Word of God, God dispatches the angels with our answer.

Matthew 7:9-11 Or what man is there of you, whom if his son ask bread, will he give him a stone? Or if he ask a fish, will he give him a serpent? If ye then, being evil, know how to give good gifts unto your children, how much more shall your Father which is in heaven give good things to them that ask him?

In this passage, Jesus parallels natural, earthly parents' desire to give their children what they request or need, to our Heavenly Father's desire to give to us what we request or need. Jesus is saying that just as we do not hold back good and needful things from our children, God will likewise not hold back any good or needful thing from us when we pray and ask Him.

So then, the question is, if we have prayed for something and have not received it, and God has released it to us, where is it? The answer is, "it's in the spiritual realm."

Ephesians 1:3 Blessed be the God and Father of our Lord Jesus Christ, who hath blessed us with all spiritual blessings "in heavenly places" in Christ.

This passage shows us what happens to our prayer request once God releases it. It's released in *"heavenly places,"* or rather, "in the spiritual realm." When we pray for something (according to the Word of God), He releases it to us. However, it is released first in the spiritual realm. Then, it's the job of the angels that war and fight on our behalf to get it to us.

First, we go before God in prayer and ask Him for it. Second, God releases the answer to our prayer in the spiritual realm to the angels to bring to us. Third, the angels carry our blessings (answers to our prayers) to us.

So if this is true, then what is it that holds up our prayers and blessings?

We all know that we are in a spiritual warfare against Satan and demon spirits. They fight against the angels to hinder us from receiving our blessings. Once we have prayed, God releases our blessings to the angels to bring to us, but the angels of God are met with hindrance and resistance by demonic opposition. So the hold up in us receiving our blessings is not God's reluctance or unwillingness to send the blessing or answered prayer to us, but the opposition or fight of demonic spirits attempting to hinder them from getting our blessings to us (*see Daniel 10:12-20 for scripture reference*).

Why is it that sometimes we can pray and get instant manifestations to our prayers, and other times we pray and it seems to take different lengths of time before we receive our manifestation?

When the Children of Israel entered the promise land, they had to fight for everything they obtained. However, there were different lengths of time of wars. There were some victories they received in a matter of moments.

Likewise in the spiritual realm, there will be different lengths of time for different prayer requests because of the resistance and hindrance of demon spirits that fight against the angels of God to keep us from receiving our blessings. There will be some (spiritual) battles in which we fight that our answer and manifestation will be instant. Some will take a few days, and others will take longer.

If the fight is fought in the spiritual realm, and the angels of God are fighting to get through to us with our blessings, is there anything we can do to help?

<u>Definitely</u>!

The more we pray and confess God's Word, the more we empower the angels to get through to us. It takes us having two things in order for the angels to get our blessings through to us, and for them to become manifested in the natural realm. First, it takes **"faith in God's Word;"** second, it takes **"the confession of God's Word."**

These two go together. One works with the other. The confession of God's Word stirs and activates our faith. And, our faith activates the Word of God. These are the two things that help to empower the angels to get through to us with our blessings.

1 Timothy 6:12 Fight the fight of faith...

While the angels are fighting in the spiritual realm, we must fight in the natural with our faith and confessions. Our faith and confession of the Word of God fuels and empowers the angels of God to continue to fight on our behalf to break through and get to us. They can only fight as long as we are fighting with our faith and confessions. When we give up the fight of our faith, they must give up the fight to break through.

It's like a car. In order for a car to be driven (if it's operating properly), it must first have gasoline to fuel the car. The Word of God is like the vehicle, and your faith is like the fuel that empowers and activates the vehicle (the Word of God when you speak it). The more gas that is pumped into the carburetor of a car, the faster the car goes. Likewise, the more you confess the Word of God, the stronger your faith will become. And, the stronger and more stable your faith becomes, the more you activate the Word.

The more you continue to confess the Word of God and stand in faith on His Word, the more you empower the angels of God (through your faith) to break through. So, once again, the angels of God fight in the spiritual realm to get to us, but we must fight the fight of faith and confessions to aid and assist them.

The Transformer

Once again, when we pray for something according to the Word of God, God releases it. It is then the job of the angels to fight on our behalf to get that Word or answered prayer to us. As we fight the fight of faith, and we are diligent and disciplined to confess the Word, we assist and empower the angels of God to get through to us.

Once the angels get through to us with the Word of our blessings, it is at that time unusable to us. We cannot utilize a spiritual blessing in the natural realm. God does not send us physical cars, houses, and material blessings from heaven. He sends them to us in the spiritual realm. But, they must first be transformed to the natural manifestation before they can become of any use to us.

It's like someone bringing you crude oil to fuel your car. Even though gasoline is a byproduct of crude oil, the crude oil would be of no use to you as fuel for your car until it could be properly refined, processed, and turned into gasoline. Likewise, once the angels have been successful in fighting and getting our answered prayer through to us, it must then be refined or changed into something we can use in the natural realm. The way that we refine or change it from the spiritual realm to the natural realm is through the transformation process of confessing the Word.

Romans 12:2 And be not conformed to this world: but be ye transformed by the renewing of your mind...

This scripture shows us how Satan desires to conform or change us to become like the world (to think, talk, and act in a carnal, worldly or sinful manner). But God is telling us to *not* allow Satan to conform or change us into the world's image, but rather, become transformed into God's image. The way that God instructs us to do this is to become "**_transformed_**" by the renewing of our minds. What transforms and renews the mind is the confession of God's Word.

You don't have to do anything to become conformed to the world, because we live in an evolving, natural, sinful world. The environment of the world is sinful and carnal. This sinful environment of the world engulfs and continually changes everything and everyone in it (that does not resist) to its conformity. If we do not do anything to combat this change, this spiritual evolutionary process will take place in our lives and will eventually change the way we think, talk, and act to the pattern and likeness of the world.

On the other hand, if we begin to diligently confess God's Word over our lives, instead of our minds, lifestyle, and actions becoming conformed to the world, they will become changed or transformed into that image (of whatever we are confessing).

It's the Word of God that transforms or changes us from thinking and acting like the world to thinking and acting like Christ. It's simple. The more we confess the Word of God over our lives, the more our minds and lives will change and line up with the Word of God. On the other hand, the less we confess the Word of God, the less our minds and lives will line up with the Word, and the more we will evolve into the image of the world and begin to talk, act, and live like the world.

So in essence, the Word of God is a "**_transformer_**." It processes, refines, transforms, and changes things. With this in mind, let's go back to what we discussed earlier. We said that once we pray according to the Word, God answers our prayer and dispatches the answer to our prayer to His angels to bring them to us. As we "**_fight the fight of_** *faith*" (through faith and confession of the Word), we empower the angels of God to break through and bring us the answer to our prayer. But when the answer arrives, it must be changed from the spiritual realm to the natural manifestation where it can be of use to us.

This is where the power and authority of our words and confessions come in place and begin to make changes for us. In our opening scripture, Proverbs 18:21, it says, *"Death and life are in the power of the tongue..."* God has given us the ability to give life to our worlds and circumstances by the words we speak. This ability to give life is actually the ability to change that which exists in the spiritual realm into the natural manifestation.

I believe that if we could look into the spiritual realm, we would be able to see many blessings that God has sent to us. But because we did not refine or transform those blessings to the natural realm where they could be of use to us, we were never able to occupy or utilize them.

I believe that there are many people who have prayed for things over and over again, which God has already sent to them by His angels. But, because of a lack of understanding about confessions, and a failure to transform those blessings from the spiritual realm to the natural manifestation (through their confessions), they failed to possess and occupy what was already sent to them.

Imagine someone praying for a new car for years. Also imagine that God had sent the answer to that prayer the first day they prayed for it, and soon afterwards it arrived by the angels. The car has been there available to them in the spiritual realm, but because they never knew it was there for them, they continued to cry out to God for it, when it had already been given to them.

It's like someone being in financial hardship. While in this hardship, someone wired a million dollars to their checking account. Although they have the money accessible to them, they would not be able to access the money unless they first of all knew they had it, and secondly, they went down to the bank and physically withdrew it. While it is in their account, it is only numbers in a bank's computer system. But if they were to go down to the bank to withdraw the money from their account, they would then be able to turn those numbers into hard cash and use it to get out of the financial hardship.

This is the situation with many of God's people. Many have been crying out to the Lord for His help and provisions. But God has already answered their prayer and wired their needs (answered prayer) to their account (by His angels). But even though what they need has been made available to them, they failed to physically possess it because of a lack of knowledge about confession, and a failure to (withdraw their needs) activate their confessions.

Don't let your blessings and answered prayers hang out there in the spiritual realm. Begin a life of confession of the Word, and take advantage of the blessings that God has released, and the angels have fought to get to you.

The Consistency of Confession

We are constantly being bombarded with Satan's attempt to conform us to the world. This is a day-by-day, hour-by-hour, minute-by-minute process. Since we encounter this non-stop attempt of Satan to evolve us into the image of the world, we must therefore go through the counter-conformation process by being continually transformed and renewed by the Word of God.

Psalms 1:2   But his <u>delight</u> is in the law of the LORD; and in his law doth he <u>meditate</u> day and night.

In this scripture, the law refers to the Word of God. But this word "meditate" has a different meaning than it appears. This word "meditate" is the Greek word "*Hagah,*" which means to mutter or speak. God is also saying that our "delight" should be in the Word. This word "delight" is the Greek word "*Sunedomai*" which means, "to have joy, pleasure and fellowship." So when you put it all together, this passage is saying that we should have a continual joy, dwelling, and fellowship in speaking or confessing the Word of God.

For many people, the only time they pray and confess the Word of God is in the morning. These people begin their day with the anointing of God and the mind of Christ, but by the end of the day (through the constant conformity of the world), the anointing has lifted, and they are just as carnal minded as the world. When you only pray and confess the Word in the morning, it's the nutritional equivalent to only eating breakfast, and not eating or drinking anything else until the next morning. Even though your body could survive with only one meal and drink of water a day, if this were all the food and water you had for the day, you would become weak, dehydrated, and nutritionally unfit. Just as we must eat and drink water throughout the day for our natural body to remain strong, healthy, and fit, we must also pray and confess the Word "throughout the day" for our spirit-man to remain strong and healthy.

In 1 Thessalonians 5:17, the Bible tells us to *"pray without ceasing."* Praying without ceasing does not mean that you pray without stopping, it simply means that you have an attitude and lifestyle of continual prayer and confessions. This passage carries the same meaning as the passage above in Psalms 1:2, which tell us to *"confess the Word day and night."*

What we are to do is to begin our day with prayer. The Lord's Prayer represents a prayer outline to which Jesus taught His disciples things they should pray for every day. There were many prayers Jesus prayed and taught His disciples, but this prayer was one in which He was instructing them on issues they should pray for and address to God each day. If Jesus is to be our example, which He is, then His pattern of prayer shows us that we should always rise early and get in the presence of God and seek His face, and petition Him for our needs and desires. God wants us to seek Him for a daily supply of our needs and essentials (*Give us this day our daily bread. Matthew 6:11*).

After Jesus prayed in the morning, you seldom find Him praying to the Father anymore throughout the day. What you find Him doing the rest of the day is speaking the Word, decreeing and declaring His Word, and through His Word showing forth signs, wonders, and miracles.

We should likewise begin our day in prayer, getting into God's presence with praise, worship, and thanksgiving. As we seek His face and get in His presence, He clothes us with His anointing. This is also a time in which we petition Him for our daily bread (our needs and desires). The rest of the day should be filled with doing what Jesus did (speaking, decreeing, and declaring the Word of God).

The morning time will not be the only time you pray. There will always be additional issues for which the Holy Spirit will prompt your heart to pray. But the morning time is the pattern to which Jesus taught us to set our hearts to pray and seek the Father. Afterwards, we are to fill our day with confessions (speaking, decreeing, and declaring His Word).

"Praying without ceasing" is to begin your day in prayer, but continue to speak, decree, and declare the Word of God throughout your day. When you do so, you give your spiritual-man its needed nutrition (from the Word of God) to stay strong throughout the day. You also counteract Satan's attempt to conform you to the world, and you transform your life, mind, and circumstances to line up with the Word, and bring into manifestation the things you are confessing.

Beginning a Life of Confessions

Begin by taking one scripture and confess it on intervals throughout your day. Let's say that one of the most prevalent areas of need in your life is finance. Look in the area of confessions that deals with financial needs or prosperity and find a scripture. Begin by confessing it at least once on your way to work, on your morning break at work, on your lunch break, on your afternoon break, on your way home from work, and before you go to bed. If you need to write it (your scripture) down, then go ahead. It will only take a few seconds to make this confession, but it will make a world of a difference in your life.

It only takes about five seconds to confess a scripture. If you confessed one scripture six times a day, it would only take about 30 seconds a day. This may seem really simple, which it is, but when you make up in your mind to become disciplined in confessing the Word, the devil will fight you in every way he can, because he knows the spiritual impact it will have on your life, and against him.

Take a different scripture dealing with a different issue or subject each day. One day it can be a script over your finances. The next day take a script for your children. The next day take a script for your health. The next day take one for your marriage (or if single, your life as a single Christian), etc.

If you have not already been confessing the Word each day, do not try to take on more than one scripture a day until you can become disciplined enough to confess that one scripture six times a day for several days. The hardest part of becoming a man or woman of confession is discipline. In the natural army, discipline is the number one attribute that is needed to become a good soldier. It's the same in the spiritual realm. If you are going to be successful in doing anything in the Kingdom of God, it is going to take discipline.

If you somehow forget to make your confession at the appointed time, make it up on your next confession interval. Try not to get off track so that you only have to make up one or two extra confessions with the next one. Don't wait until the end of the day and try to make up all of them. This would somewhat defeat the purpose. The purpose is to get your soul to become disciplined in confessing the Word throughout the day. Your soul is like a child. It doesn't want to confess the Word. But just as you must teach a child to become disciplined through redundancy to do something, you must also do the same with your soul. Even though it seems simple, the first week will seem like pulling teeth, but soon, it will become second nature.

Once you have been successful in disciplining yourself to confess one scripture, believe God for not only one scripture, but to also add more scriptures to your times of confession. Build on your time until you can take two or three minutes (or more) at each interval and confess the Word. If you made your prayer confessions for two minutes, six times a day, that would only total twelve minutes a day.

Just think about it: Twelve minutes a day for something that will change your way of thinking (give you the mind of Christ), transform your life, and bring the manifestations of God's blessings in your life. Considering the fact that the average Christian watches on average at least an hour and a half of television (90 minutes) each day, twelve minutes is not much time at all.

* **Note**: I have a simple principal that helps me to remain disciplined in prayer and confessions. Remember, I said earlier that our soul is like a child that must be trained and taught. When we are teaching and training our children, one of the principals we often teach them is that in order for them to receive something good, they must have done their chores. We do not (or at least should not) reward our children with fun, privileges, and pleasures until they have been diligent in accomplishing their chores and duties. I discipline my soul somewhat the same way.

I do not allow my soul the privilege and pleasure of watching non-Christian television or movies unless it has done the chore and duties of prayer, study, and confessions that day. To some, this may sound somewhat childish, but again, remember, our soul is like that of a child. So, since my soul wants the pleasure of watching a few minutes of television and sports highlights at the end of the day, it is less fervent to fight and war against my spirit when it is time to pray, study, and make confessions.

Once you have become disciplined in staying with your daily interval confessions, try to add a time of confessions after you have prayed and petitioned the Lord in the morning. After you have spent quality time in the presence of God in worship, praise, thanksgiving, and petition, try to take about five to ten extra minutes (or more) with confessions. This can consist of general confessions covering a variety of areas in your life, or they can also pertain to one particular area in which you may be experiencing trouble.

When you go to bed at night, don't go to bed watching television. After you have prayed (before going to sleep), take a scripture and first confess it a few times, then meditate on it for a few moments. This will help to cleanse your spirit of all the garbage you were watching on television, or chaos you may have experienced throughout your day, and allow you to sleep and rest in the peace of God.

Daily scripture confessions will not only transform your mind, life, and circumstances, they will also help your prayer life, as well as add to your scripture knowledge, memory, and vocabulary.

Counteracting Satan's Onslaught

We said earlier that we are constantly being bombarded by Satan's attempt to conform us to the world. We also said that unless we counteract Satan's onslaught, we will eventually evolve into the likeness of the world. For every attack of Satan upon our minds, we should respond with a counter-attack of the Word.

People always quote James 4:7, which says, "*...Resist the devil, and he will flee from you.*" some think that the way we resist the devil is through sheer will. Although your *will* is ultimately the part of you that will either give in to, or stand against the devil, your *will* can easily be influenced by Satan.

Our soul consists of the mind, the emotions, and the will. If Satan can sway your mind and emotions in a particular way, your *will* soon will follow. So our resistance to Satan's attacks should not merely rely on our will to resist him, but on something else.

Matthew 4:3-11 And when the tempter came to him, he said, If thou be the Son of God, command that these stones be made bread. But he answered and said, it is written, man shall not live by bread alone, but by every Word that proceedeth out of the mouth of God. Then the devil taketh him up into the holy city, and setteth him on a pinnacle of the temple, and saith unto him, If thou be the Son of God, cast thyself down: for it is written, He shall give his angels charge concerning thee: and in their hands they shall bear thee up, lest at any time thou dash thy foot against a stone. Jesus said unto him, It is written again, Thou shalt not tempt the Lord thy God.

Again, the devil taketh him up into an exceeding high mountain, and showeth him all the kingdoms of the world, and the glory of them; And saith unto him, All these things will I give thee, if thou wilt fall down and worship me. Then saith Jesus unto him, Get thee hence, Satan: for it is written, Thou shalt worship the Lord thy God, and him only shalt thou serve. Then the devil leaveth him, and, behold, angels came and ministered unto him.

In this passage, we find Satan attacking Jesus' soul, much the same way that he attacks us. Whether he speaks to us in an audible voice, or through the voice of temptation, seduction, or deceit, it is still the same voice. We are to resist and counteract his attacks on our soul the same way Jesus did. With each of these temptations, Jesus resisted Satan and counteracted his attacks by saying, "*it is written...*" In other words, He resisted and counteracted each of Satan's attacks by speaking the Word of God.

Every time Satan tempts or attack us, we are to also resist and counteract his words with the Word of God. Whether it's an attack that brings anger, lust, bitterness, or any other spirit upon us, or whether it's an attack upon our health, finances, or any other area of our lives, we are to do like Jesus did and aggressively launch a counterattack of the Word of God for every one of his attacks and temptations.

When Satan speaks to us, he is attempting to plant a seed. If we fail to counteract his seeds, they will eventually grow and give place to the devil and create demonic strongholds in our lives. But the Bible tells us in Ephesians 4:27 to "*Give no place to the devil.*" If we do not counteract his satanic seeds and we allow them to grow, we are giving place to the devil. However, the Word of God is also a (much more powerful) seed.

When we confess the seed of the Word of God, we are planting the blessings of God into our hearts, minds and lives. And, not only are we planting good things when we confess the Word, the Word of God also root up, pluck out, and cut off every negative seed planted by Satan.

So as you go through your day, when Satan speaks to your heart, don't just let him plant seeds of destruction that will grow and spring up into wicked and unwanted things in your heart and life. Instead, do like Jesus did, and resist and counteract his negative seeds with the seed of the Word of God. And, when you counteract Satan's seed with the seed of the Word, you bring about God's blessings in your life. This will also help you to pull up and root out negative seeds, so that they will not work or prosper against you.

This book is a book of confessions on just about every subject. Whatever area of your life which Satan is attacking, turn to that section and begin to resist him and launch a counterattack with the Word, which will bring forth strength, deliverance, and the manifestation of God's blessings.

The Difference Between Prayer and Confession

In prayer, we often intermingle praying and confession. Prayer is often considered confessing the Word, and confessing the Word is often considered prayer. Even though we use each one interchangeably, there is a difference.

Prayer is simply to communicate with or talk to God. Prayer often consists of us asking or petitioning God for something. Even though requesting and petitioning God for something is the most often form of communication we have with God, it is not necessarily the only forms of communication with Him.

The "prayer of praise" is not a prayer in which we petition God for anything. It's a prayer in which we only give Him praise, adoration, and worship. There is also the prayer of thanksgiving. It's also a prayer in which we do not ask God for anything. It's a prayer in which we simply give thanks to God for His blessings upon our lives.

In the prayer of petition, we specifically ask God for His provisions, help and deliverance. **In confession, we do not pray and ask God to do something for us or give something to us. Instead, we exercise His authority that He has already given to us to speak, decree, and declare it ourselves**. To some, this may sound the same. In fact, it almost looks the same, but there is a difference.

For example: If you were ill and needing healing, you may pray something like this: **Father, Your Word says that you would heal me of all of my sickness and diseases. So I pray therefore that you would heal me of this sickness and infirmity that is against me by Your power**

and might...

Notice, in this prayer request above, the person praying is asking God to heal them. They correctly followed the pattern of prayer by praying the Word of God, and they made a request to God for their healing. However, if you were confessing the Word of God concerning your healing, it may sound something like this:

I confess the Word of God over my body that I am healed by the stripes of Jesus Christ. I decree that this weapon of sickness that has been formed against my body can no longer prosper, and I speak healing and good health unto my body.

Notice the difference between the two. In the first prayer (praying), the person praying clearly asks God to do the healing. In the second one (confession), the person doing the confession did not ask God to do the healing at all; they simply exercised their authority that God has given them to speak, decree, and declare His Word.

When a baby gets hungry, the parents not only buy the food for the baby, but they also prepare the food and feed it to their baby. As the baby matures into a young child, the parents still provide the food for their child, but there comes a time when the child grows and becomes able to feed him or herself. Later, they even mature to a place where they can even prepare their own meal. The parents are still ultimately the provider of the food, but they have now given to their child the knowledge, permission (authority) and resources to prepare it themselves.

It's the same way with God. He has given us (as mature men and women of God) the power and authority to speak, decree, and declare according to His Word what we need in our lives (prepare our own meal). He is still the ultimate provider. He is still the power and source of our authority, and we must spend quality time with Him in prayer and in His Word every day to maintain that power. If you take the power source away from the object of power, that object will eventually lose its power, because it no longer has a source.

We are to follow the pattern of prayer that Jesus taught us. This pattern is to spend quality time in the presence of the Father and diligently seek His face each day for our source. Then, we are to begin to do what Jesus did the remainder of our day, which is not to ask and beg God to do the work for us, but begin to confess God's Word—decreeing and declaring it ourselves over our lives and our circumstances.

Matthew 16:19   And I will give unto thee the keys of the kingdom of heaven: and whatsoever thou shalt bind on earth shall be bound in heaven: and whatsoever thou shalt loose on earth shall be loosed in heaven.

In this passage, Jesus is teaching about the power, dominion, and authority that God has given us through His Word to bind and loose. Notice, He did not say for us to pray that God would bind and loose the devil for us, but for "*us*" to rather utilize the keys (the authority) that He has already given us to bind and loose the devil ourselves. The emphasis in this passage is not on God doing the binding, but for us to do it.

We not only bind Satan with our words when we say, "I bind you Satan," we also bind Satan with our confession of the Word of God. Because, when we speak the Word of God in our confessions, we automatically bind the devil with the authority and power we have in the spoken Word of God.

God is looking for us as men and women of God to begin to walk in the dominion and authority that He has already given us. This place of authority is when we begin to walk in our divine (God-like) authority.

Remember, God created us in His image and His likeness. The image of God represents our three-part being of spirit, soul and body. But the likeness of God represents our ability and authority as, "a speaking spirit," like God, to speak and declare—and have our words come to pass.

There is a time to pray and petition God for our needs, wants, and desires. But there also comes a time (of confession) when we should begin to walk in our divine authority and speak, decree, and declare our needs, wants, and desires ourselves.

We spend all our time praying and asking God to do something that He has already given us the authority to do. We begin by praying and asking God to bless us. But God is looking for us as believers to begin to exercise the authority that He has given us through His Word to speak, decree, and declare His Word ourselves.

In short, when you pray and ask God to do it for you, it is prayer. Confession is when you exercise your authority (through faith) that God has already given to you to speak, decree, and declare His Word yourself.

* **PLEASE NOTE:** Prayer and confession can be done at the same time. In our prayer handbook series, "The Weapons of Our Warfare, Volumes I & II," prayers often contain prayer and confession. Many of the prayers begin with petitioning God, and later changes to decreeing that particular thing. They were intentionally joined together to cover all bases of prayer and confession. However, even with these prayers, confession is still needed.

Biblical Examples
of Confessing the Word

Now that we understand what confessions are, let's look at a few scriptures that relate with confession.

Psalms 107:2 <u>*Let the redeemed of the LORD say so,*</u> *whom he hath redeemed from the hand of the enemy.*

The redeemed that God is referring to in this passage are those who have received Jesus Christ into their hearts and lives, become born-again, and as a result, become redeemed from the curse of the law and the punishment of hell through the blood of Jesus Christ.

If you are a born-again believer, then you are the redeemed to which God is referring. But notice, God did not say for the redeemed to request it, ask or beg for it, or pray for it. It simply says for the redeemed to *"say so."* To *say so* is to simply speak, confess, decree and declare that it *"is so!"* God is looking for us to begin to *"say so"* regarding our situations and circumstances. And, as we continue to *"say so,"* we will begin to see transformation and change.

Ecclesiastes 8:4   Where the word of a king is, there is power...

As believers, God has ordained each of us as kings. Jesus Christ is the great, Most High King, over us—the little kings. God has also ordained us as kings to rule and reign. This passage is telling us that a king has power in His words. As kings, God has given us the power and authority to change things with our words. There is no other creature on earth with this power and authority but (the saved, regenerated, born-again Christian) man. We have the power to transform our worlds (situations and circumstances) by the words we speak.

Romans 4:17 (As it is written, I have made thee a father of many nations,) before him whom he believed, even God, who quickeneth the dead, and "calleth those things which be not as though they were."

This passage expresses another parameter of confessions. In confessions, you call or confess things that are not (according to the Word of God in your life) as though they were (according to the Word of God in your life). Because, when you call or speak them according to the Word of God, they become transformed and changed to what you speak.

Psalms 91:2 "I will say of the LORD," He is my refuge and my fortress: my God; in him will I trust.

David said, "*I will say of the Lord*," meaning that we should say or confess what the Lord says (though His Word) about our circumstances and situations, rather than the way they appear to be in the natural realm.

2 Corinthians 4:18 While we look not at the things which are seen, but at the things which are not seen: for the things which are seen are temporal; but the things which are not seen are eternal.

Notice it says that the things which are seen (meaning things in the physical, natural realm) are things that are temporal. The definition of this word "temporal" is something that is temporary, changeable, or subject to change. What makes them subject to change is the Word of God. When natural, physical things become subjected to the Word of God (through confession), it causes them to change and become transformed to your confession.

Joel 3:10 ...let the weak say, I am strong.

In this familiar passage, it is saying that if you are weak, instead of confessing that you are weak, begin to confess that you are strong. This word "weak" does not only apply to physical or spiritual weakness, it also refers to any type of insufficiency in your life. So if your finances are insufficient to meet your needs, then your finances are "weak." If you are sick or ill, then your health is insufficient or weak. So then, whatever area of your life that you experience lack or insufficiency, God is giving you His authority to speak His Word and change or transform them.

So, if it's spiritual or physical strength you need, begin to confess, "I am strong." If you are weak in your finances, begin to confess, "My finances are strong." If you are ill or weak in your health, you can begin to confess that you are healed, in good health, and your health is strong.

This scripture didn't say to pray that God would help you to become strong, but for you to decree, declare, and confess that you are strong. Again, when we speak the Word of God, it transforms the spiritual to the natural manifestation. So if you are weak or have insufficiency, as you confess the Word of God, your weakness or insufficiency will become transformed into strength and sufficiency, and your need will be met and manifested in your life.

If you notice, none of the scriptures above involve praying and asking God to do anything. They all involve a principle of confession that God wants to bring His people to, which is to exercise the authority that He has given to us, and begin to decree and declare His Word ourselves.

* It is recommended that you get the book, "**Praying in Your Divine Authority**." This book will give you a better

understanding of who you truly are in Christ, and the divine authority that God has given you through Christ. Once you confidently gain this understanding, you will be able to more boldly speak, decree and declare God's Word, and it will give you a better understanding of your authority, dominion, and power over Satan.

Section II

*Authority
Confession*

Introduction to Authority Confession

The first confession in this book is a confession of your authority in Christ. The reason why I placed this confession first is because it is needful in prayer warfare. Satan knows that his weapons are powerless against us as believers. So he uses the only tools that he can use against us to hinder or slow us down, which are doubt, fear, and unbelief.

In order for us to effectively war against Satan, we must have faith in the following:

1. We must have faith in the Word of God.
2. We must have faith in God's willingness and ability to perform His Word on our behalf.
3. We must have faith in who we are in Christ.
4. We must have faith in our authority to decree and declare God's Word.

Most people have no problem with the first two points above, but many Christians fail to operate in the last two points. Many fail to operate in faith in who they are in Christ, and in their authority to decree and declare the Word of God. And, often times when they do, their level of faith in these two areas waiver back and forth like a feather in the wind.

James 1:6-8 But let him ask in faith, nothing wavering. For he that wavereth is like a wave of the sea driven with the wind and tossed. For let not that man think that he shall receive any thing of the Lord. A double minded man is unstable in all his ways.

When we fail to operate in these two areas, or waiver

in faith, we allow the devil to use his tools of doubt, fear and unbelief against us, which assassinates our faith and hinders our prayers and confessions.

It is important that you not only fight with the Word, but that you also fight with your faith. You must not only have faith in God's Word and God's ability and willingness to help you, you must also have faith (and confidence) in who you are in Christ, and your authority and power you have to decree and declare the Word of God.

As you confess this type of confession, it will keep you from wavering, help build up your faith and confidence in who you are in Christ, and give you the faith and confidence you need to decree God's Word and successfully war against Satan.

I suggest that you rehearse this scripture confession at least every two or three days. Continue with your regular prayer and specific faith confessions each day, but make this confession along with them every two or three days. As you do so, it will help charge and stabilize your faith in who you are in Christ, and your ability and authority to represent Him in decreeing and declaring His Word—thereby giving the devil "*no place*" to hinder or stop you.

Authority Confession

I am the righteousness of God created in Christ Jesus. I'm created in the image of God. I'm created in His likeness, which is His authority and power. I am God's ambassador and His representative in the earth realm. I represent Him in power and authority. I walk in the power of God. I walk in the authority of God, and I walk in divine dominion.

I have God's Spirit upon me. His power and His presence exude through me. Jesus Christ is the anointed one by God, and He has placed His anointing upon my life. Therefore, I am also anointed—with a double portion. And because I am anointed, I have the authority and power of God to loose the bands of wickedness, to undo and remove burdens, to let the oppressed go free, and to break and destroy every yoke of the devil from my life, and from the lives of others.

Jesus Christ has given me the keys to the kingdom, which is the power and authority of His Word. Therefore, whatever I bind in the earth is bound in the spiritual realm, and whatever I loose in the earth is loosed in the spiritual realm. So I walk in divine authority, and in the binding and loosening power of Jesus Christ.

Jesus gave me the authority to use His name. Therefore, in the name of the Lord Jesus Christ, as I bind principalities, powers, rulers of the darkness of this world, and spiritual wickedness in high places, they are therefore bound in the heavens, and bound in the earth. And, they are helpless, powerless, inoperative and ineffective against me, and against the Word of God that I speak.

I have authority according to the Word of God to speak

to my mountains. And according to the Word of the Living God, whatever mountains I speak to and command to be removed, they must obey me and be removed, uprooted, and cast into the sea.

I am the redeemed of the Lord. Whatever I say or confess to be so according to the Word of God, "*is so.*" And whatever I have said (according to God's Word), *is so*, and comes to pass. So whatever I say, decree, and declare according to God's Word concerning healing, health, peace, prosperity, safety, or any of God's blessings, "*is so*," and comes to pass.

I believe in the Word of God. I trust in the Word, and I confidently stand upon the Word of God. I am what the Word says I am, and I can do what the Word says I can do. I have (by faith) the blessings of the Lord upon my life that the Word declares are mine.

I am a doer of the Word, and not just a hearer. My confessions fall in line with the Word. My faith falls in line with the Word; therefore, my life, health, finances, thoughts, situations, circumstances, actions, and works also fall in line with the Word.

As I speak the Word of God, they are no longer my words, but God's Words. And therefore, the Word of God that I speak cannot and shall not return void, but it shall accomplish and strike the mark of that in which it is sent (through my prayer and confessions) to perform.

I do not focus on the (negative) things that are seen. Those things are temporal (and subject to change). I see by revelation into the spiritual realm, and I focus upon those things (according to the Word of God) which are unseen. For I am a man/woman of faith; I am justified by faith; I speak by faith; I believe by faith; I see by faith; and I therefore have an expectation to receive what I have prayed for and confessed by faith. For I walk by faith, and I live by faith, and not by sight.

God has given me a commission to take back from the devil what he has stolen from me. The Kingdom of heaven allows violence in the spiritual realm against the forces of darkness. I don't ask the devil for anything. I don't beg him to do anything. I am the violent, and with the power and authority of Jesus Christ, I take by force the things that belong to me.

I confess that everywhere I go that signs follow me. For the Word of God has declared to me that these signs follow them that believe. And because I am a believer, I receive miracles, signs, and wonders following me, exemplifying that I am a believer who has been washed by the blood of Jesus Christ, and filled with His Holy Spirit.

By the power and authority of Jesus Christ, these signs follow me: I cast out demons and devils; I speak with new tongues; I lay hands upon the sick, and they do recover.

My weapons of prayer and confession of the Word of God are not carnal, but mighty through God. With the authority of the Word of God through Christ Jesus, I pull down strongholds; I cast down imaginations, and every high thing that exalts itself against the knowledge of God. And I bring into captivity every unrighteous, immoral, and ungodly thought to the obedience of Christ.

By the authority of God in the name of Jesus Christ, I tread upon Satan as the lion, the adder, the young lion, and as the dragon. I tread upon every demon and demonic spirit as serpents and scorpions. I tread over all the powers and forces of the enemy, and nothing that the enemy launches against me or my family can harm or hurt us in any way.

Jesus Christ is seated in heavenly places with all things under His feet. I am hid in Christ in heavenly places. And because I am in Christ, all things are also under my feet. And in the name of Jesus Christ, every demonic principality, power, ruler of darkness of this world, and spiritual wickedness in high places are all under my feet.

Jesus Christ conquered and triumphed in victory over Satan and demonic principalities and powers. And since I am in Christ, I am also more than a conqueror over all principalities and powers. For (through Christ) I am victorious, and I walk in total and complete victory in every area of my life.

I abide in Christ, and Christ abides in me. For I am the temple of the Holy Ghost. Therefore, greater is Jesus Christ who lives, rules, reigns, dwells within, and empowers me, than the enemy that is against me in the world.

God created me in His likeness to rule, reign, and dominate in the earth. For God has anointed me as a king. I am a king unto the most High King, Jesus Christ. And where the word of a king is, there is power and authority. As a king, I walk in God's power. I walk in God's authority, and in God's dominion. As a king, whatever I decree and declare in the spiritual realm is established and manifested in the physical realm. So as a king, I make these declarations: Sickness, disease, poverty, lack, and insufficiency, are all under my feet.

As a king, I rule and reign over them. And whatever I dictate and command them to do, they must obey me and follow what I say. I speak to sickness now, and I command you to get under my feet. I speak to lack and insufficiency now, and I command you to get under my feet. I speak to every trouble in my life, and I command you to cease, now. I speak to every storm in my life, and I command you to be at peace, and be still, now, in the name of Jesus Christ!

As a king, I decree that every promise in the Word of God is mine. They belong to me. I receive every one of them unto my life. And I decree that no demonic spirit is able to hinder or stop me from receiving any of my blessings.

As a king unto Jesus Christ, I also rule and reign over every devil, demon, demonic spirit, demonic force, and principality. And as a king unto Christ Jesus, I decree and declare them to be off limits to my life, and to the lives of my family. I am the anointed of God, and I command every evil and demonic spirit to touch not God's anointed. I forbid and prohibit them from touching anything that belongs to me. I also forbid and prohibit them from touching the lives of my family (in any way), or anyone who is related to me.

As a king, I decree that only the will of God is done in my life. I decree that Satan's will of killing, stealing, and destruction is prohibited and bound from my life. Only the will of God, which is to give me life, and life more abundantly is performed and manifested in my life.

I declare that because I am a child of God, that God is for me. And since God is for me, then no person, devil, demonic spirit, force, or principality can stand against me, nor can they come against me and succeed. I also declare that no weapon that Satan forms against me can hinder me, nor can they prosper against me in any way—spiritually, physically, financially, socially, or emotionally. For God is my shield and my buckler, and His angels are encamped around my life and the lives of my family to protect us, and keep us in all of our ways.

I now choose to walk in my authority and dominion as a king. I put on the helmet of salvation—knowing who I am in Christ, and knowing who Christ is in me and through me. I am rooted, settled and established in my faith in Christ, and in my position of authority in Him. And as I speak, decree and declare the Word of God, it cannot be stopped, hindered or hampered by the enemy.

In the name of Jesus Christ I decree it, AMEN!

Scriptures Used in the Authority Confession

2 Corinthians 5:21
Genesis 1:26-27
Psalms 92:10
Luke 4:18
2 Kings 2:9
Isaiah 58:6
Matthew 16:19
John 14:13
Ephesians 6:12
Matthew 21:21
Psalms 107:2
James 1:22
2 Corinthians 4:18
Isaiah 55:11
Romans 1:17
Romans 3:28
2 Corinthians 5:7
Matthew 11:12
Mark 16:17-18
Luke 10:20
2 Corinthians 10:4-5
Psalms 91:13
Luke 10:19

Ephesians 2:6
Psalms 8:6
2 Corinthians 2:14-15
1 Corinthians 15:57
1 John 5:4
Romans 8:37
John 15:7
1 Corinthians 3:16
1 John 4:4
Revelation 1:6
Genesis 1:26-27
Ecclesiastes 8:4
Job 22:28
Psalms 8:6
Mark 4:39
Isaiah 54:17
1 Chronicles 16:22
Matthew 16:19
John 10:10
Romans 8:31
Psalms 91:11-14
Isaiah 55:11

Section III

Confessions

Confessions of
Praise and Worship

♦ Great is the Lord and greatly to be praised. He is to be honored, and given glory above all others, and above all else. *I Chronicles 16:25*

♦ I shall give unto the Lord all the glory due unto His name, and I shall bring an offering and sacrifice before Him of worship and praise in the beauty of holiness. *I Chronicles 16:29*

♦ The Lord is great! He is all power, the glory, the victory, and the majesty. For all that is in the heavens and in the earth is the Lord's. He is the great King of all, and He is exalted as head above all. *I Chronicles 29:11*

♦ Both riches and honor come from the Lord. He reigns over all. In His hands is all power and might. He has the power to make men great, and to give strength unto all. *I Chronicles 29:12*

♦ The Lord has bought me with the price of His own blood. Therefore, I shall glorify the Lord in my body and in my spirit, which is the Lord's. *I Corinthians 6:20*

♦ In all things (in everything I do), I will give thanks unto the Lord. For this is the will of God in Christ Jesus. *I Thessalonians 5:18*

♦ Praise, honor, and glory be unto the King, who is eternal, immortal, and invisible. He is the only wise God, and He deserves the honor and glory forever and ever. *I Timothy 1:17*

♦ Jesus Christ is the King of all kings, and He is the Lord of all lords. *I Timothy 6:1*

♦ I will give continual thanksgiving and praise unto the Lord my God for His unspeakable gift of Jesus Christ our Lord. *II Corinthians 9:15*

♦ I love the Lord my God with all of my heart, all my soul, all my strength, and all of my might. *Deuteronomy 6:5*

♦ The Lord is far above all principalities, powers, mights, and dominions. His name is far above every name that is named, not only in this world, but also in that which is to come. *Ephesians 1:21*

♦ I give thanks always for all things unto God the Father, in the name of our Lord, Jesus Christ. *Ephesians 5:20*

♦ The Lord is the great "*I am that I am.*" For He is everything that I need. *Exodus 3:14*

♦ I shall bring an offering of sacrifice and praise unto the Lord continually; and the fruit of my lips shall forever give Him praise and thanksgiving. *Hebrews 13:15*

♦ The name of the Lord is Wonderful, Counselor, the Mighty God, the Everlasting Father, and the Prince of Peace. *Isaiah 9:6*

♦ There is none like the Lord in all the earth. For the Lord is great, and His name is Great and Mighty. *Jeremiah 10:6*

♦ Jesus is the great Bread of Life unto my soul. *John 6:35*

♦ The mercies of the Lord never cease. For they are

new and renewed for us every morning. Great is the faithfulness of the Lord. *Lamentations 3:23*

♦ Unto the Lord is the Kingdom, and the power, and the glory, forever and ever. *Matthew 6:13*

♦ God has highly exalted His Son—our Lord and Savior, Jesus Christ. And He has given Him a name above every name. *Philippians 2:9*

♦ I willfully and joyfully serve the Lord with gladness. I come continually before His presence with praise, songs of worship, and thanksgiving. For the Lord, *He* is God. He has made us, and not we ourselves. We are His people, and the sheep of His pasture. *Psalms 100:3*

♦ I will (daily) enter into the gates of the Lord with thanksgiving, and into His courts with praise. I will spend time each day giving thanks unto Him, and I will forever praise and bless the name of the Lord. *Psalms 100:4*

♦ The Lord is good. His mercy is everlasting, and His truth endures forever. *Psalms 100:5*

♦ I will bless the Lord from the depths of my soul. And with all that is within me, I will glorify Him, magnify Him, give Him praise, and bless His holy name. *Psalms 103:1*

♦ I will bless the Lord from the depths of my soul, and I shall not forget any of His benefits. For the Lord is the one who forgives all of my iniquities; He heals all of my sickness and diseases; He saves and redeems me from every destruction and attack against my life; He blesses me with good things, and He renews my life, health and strength, like the eagle. *Psalms 103:1-5*

♦ From the rising of the sun to the going down of the

same, the name of the Lord is worthy to be praised. *Psalms 113:3*

♦ The Lord is high above all nations, and His glory is above the heavens. *Psalms 113:4*

♦ The mercies of the Lord endure forever. For He alone has done great wonders. By His wisdom, He made the heavens. He stretched out the earth above the waters. He made the sun to shine in the day, and He made the moon and stars to shine in the night. *Psalms 136:4-9*

♦ My prayers shall be as a sweet smelling incense before the Lord, and the lifting of my hand shall be as the evening sacrifice unto Him. *Psalms 141:2*

♦ I shall speak of the glory of the Lord and talk of His power forever. *Psalms 145:11*

♦ The Kingdom of the Lord is from everlasting to everlasting, and His dominion endures throughout all times and generations. *Psalms 145:13*

♦ Great is the Lord and greatly to be praised. His greatness is unsearchable and will never end. *Psalms 145:3*

♦ Many shall speak of the mighty acts of the Lord, and I shall be one who will always declare His greatness. *Psalms 145:6*

♦ In the presence of the Lord is the fullness of joy. And at His right hand there are pleasures forevermore. *Psalms 16:11*

♦ I will continually call upon the name of the Lord: For He is worthy to be praised. *Psalms 18:3*

♦ The Lord lives, and He shall live forever and ever; blessed be my Rock, and let the God of my salvation be exalted. *Psalms 18:46*

♦ The Lord is more desirable than fine gold, and He is sweeter than the honey in a honeycomb. *Psalms 19:10*

♦ The goodness and mercy of the Lord shall surely follow me all the days of my life, and I shall dwell in the house, and in the presence of the Lord forever. *Psalms 23:6*

♦ I will give the glory to the Lord that is due unto His name, and I will worship Him in the beauty of holiness. *Psalms 29:2*

♦ I will command my soul to bless the Lord at all times, and I will command my mouth to give Him praise continually. *Psalms 34:1*

♦ The Lord is exalted above the heavens, and His glory is exalted above the earth. *Psalms 57:5*

♦ I will bless the Lord as long as I shall live, and I will lift up my hands unto His name. *Psalms 63:4*

♦ How awesome and excellent is the name of the Lord in the earth. For His glory is set above the heavens. *Psalms 8:1*

♦ The heavens belong to the Lord; the earth and fullness thereof also belong to Him. For He has created and established them both. *Psalms 89:11*

♦ There is no one in the heavens that can be compared unto the Lord; neither is there anyone among men that is like Him. *Psalms 89:6*

♦ God is great, and greatly to be reverenced and revered in the assembly of the saints. *Psalms 89:7*

♦ There is no one who is strong like the Lord God of hosts. For His faithfulness is round about us. *Psalms 89:8*

♦ The Lord rules the raging sea. And when the waves rise, He commands them to be still. *Psalms 89:9*

♦ It is a good thing to give thanksgiving unto the Lord, and to sing praises unto His name. For the Lord shows us His loving kindness in the morning, and He shows forth His faithfulness every evening. *Psalms 92:1-2*

♦ The Lord is a great God, and He is King above all other gods. *Psalms 95:3*

♦ I will continually worship, bow down, and kneel before the Lord—who is my maker. *Psalms 95:6*

♦ I will declare the glory of the Lord, and I will declare His wonders among all people. *Psalms 96:3*

♦ Honor and majesty belong to the Lord; strength and beauty are His sanctuary. *Psalms 96:6*

♦ I will worship the Lord in the beauty of His holiness; I shall reverence Him in all the earth. *Psalms 96:9*

♦ Jesus Christ is the Alpha and Omega. He is the first and the last. He is the beginning and the end. He is the one who is, the one who was, and the one who is soon to come. *Revelations 1:8*

Confessions
For Your Marriage

◆ I confess that my spouse and I speak the same thing (walk in unity), and there is no division among us. I confess that we are also perfectly joined together in the same mind (walking in agreement), and the same spirit. *I Corinthians 1:10*

◆ In the name of Jesus Christ, I confess these things over my marriage: I confess that my spouse and I walk together in love; our love is patient and long; we are kind towards one another; we are not envious towards one another; we do not behave unseemly towards one another; we do not seek to please ourselves, but to please the other; we do not provoke one another, nor do we think evil of one another; and we are faithful to one another. *I Corinthians 13:4-5*

◆ Above all things, my spouse and I have love for one another. And it's the love we share for one another that covers a multitude of faults and mistakes between us. *I Peter 4:8*

◆ By the authority of God in the name of Jesus Christ, I cast down every imagination that is against my marriage in my mind or in my spouse's mind. I cast down every high thing that attempts to exalt itself between us. And I bring into captivity (by the authority of God's Word) every thought (that is against the will of God for my marriage) to the obedience of Christ. *II Corinthians 10:5*

◆ I confess that my love for my spouse, and my spouse's love for me are renewed day by day for one another. *II Corinthians 4:16*

♦ It is God's desire for my spouse and I that we prosper, and have a happy, healthy, and successful marriage, even as we prosper spiritually. *III John 1:2*

♦ I confess that my marriage is grounded and settled in love, and shall not be moved away. *Colossians 1:23*

♦ I confess the Word of God over my marriage that there is no bitterness or strife between us; neither is there any anger, fussing, fighting, evil speaking, malice, or any ill-will towards each other. *Ephesians 4:31*

♦ I confess the Word of God that my spouse and I are kind towards one another; we are tenderhearted towards one another, and we forgive one another, even as God (for Christ sake) has forgiven us. *Ephesians 4:32*

♦ I have departed from my father and mother, and I am joined together with my spouse. We are therefore now one flesh in one spirit with Christ. *Ephesians 5:31*

♦ The Lord shall contend with every person and every spirit that comes against my marriage. *Isaiah 49:25*

♦ I decree that no weapon that is formed against my marriage (spiritually or physically) shall be able to prosper against us in any way. And every word that is spoken against us shall fall to the ground. For this is the heritage that I have as a servant of the Lord, and my righteousness is of Him. *Isaiah 54:17*

♦ As I pray and confess the Word of God over my marriage, my marriage shall be healed. For the effectual and fervent prayer of a righteous man or woman of God avails much. *James 5:16*

♦ The thief (Satan) comes to kill, steal, and destroy my marriage. But Christ (who is greater) has come to give life unto my marriage, and, the abundant life of happiness, joy and peace. *John 10:10*

♦ The Lord is able to keep my marriage and our love for one another from falling. He is also able to present us faultless before the presence of His glory with exceeding joy. *Jude 1:24*

♦ I confess that my love is renewed for my spouse every morning, and the love of my spouse is also renewed for me every morning. *Lamentations 3:23*

♦ The Lord has rebuked the devourer from my marriage; therefore, Satan has no place in my marriage, and he cannot destroy the fruit of our love, peace, or joy. *Malachi 3:11*

♦ I confess that neither my spouse nor I will take (accept or receive) any thoughts of the devil of infidelity or unfaithfulness of any kind. Neither will we ever take (accept or receive) any thoughts of separation or divorce. But we will only take the thoughts of God towards one another of love, joy, peace, long-suffering, gentleness, goodness, faith, meekness, and temperance. *Matthew 6:25, Galatians 5:22-23*

♦ It is the Lord who has joined my spouse and I together in marriage. Therefore, since God has joined us together, I decree that no person, spirit, force, or power shall be able to separate or divide us. *Matthew 19:6*

♦ I confess that my spouse and I esteem each other better than ourselves. *Philippians 2:3*

♦ I confess that my marriage (and our love for each other) is like a tree that is planted by the rivers of water, that bring forth blessed and prosperous fruit in its season. The leaves of our marriage (our love, happiness, joy and peace) shall not wither, and whatsoever we do together shall prosper. *Psalms 1:3*

♦ I confess that the Lord continually renews the youth, excitement, and passion of my marriage, like He renews the strength of the eagle. *Psalms 103:5*

♦ The Lord perfects (takes care of) those things that concern me about my marriage. *Psalms 138:8*

♦ The Lord gives instructions to my spouse and I concerning our marriage. He teaches us the right things to do, and He guides us continually with His eyes. *Psalms 32:8*

♦ As I trust in the Lord, and commit the ways of my marriage unto Him (through prayer and confession), He brings them to pass. *Psalms 37:5*

♦ The Lord shall deliver my marriage from every snare of the enemy, and from every attack against us. *Ps. 91:3*

♦ I confess that my spouse and I are kind to each other, affectionate towards one another, in love with each other, and we honor and respect one another. *Romans 12:10*

♦ I confess that my marriage shall not be overcome with evil towards one another, but we shall (through Christ) overcome evil with love. *Romans 12:21*

♦ I confess that my marriage is not conformed to the world's view and image for marriage. But I confess that my marriage is transformed to God's view and will for my marriage by the renewing of our minds through the Word of God. For this is the good, acceptable, and perfect will of God. *Romans 12:2*

Confessions
For Your Children

♦ My children are a heritage unto the Lord. They belong to the Lord; therefore, Satan cannot have them, and neither can he have any place in their lives. *Psalms 127:3*

♦ The Lord is faithful. He has established my children, and He shall keep them from all evil. *II Thessalonians 3:3*

♦ I confess that my children do not follow that which is evil or wrong, but they follow that which is good, wholesome, and godly. *III John 1:11*

♦ It is God's desire above all things for my children that they prosper, have success, and walk in divine health, even as they prosper spiritually. *III John 1:2*

♦ I confess that all of my children are saved, born-again, and living for the Lord. For He has promised me in His Word that He would save my entire house (including all of my children). *Acts 11:14*

♦ I confess that my children have believed and received the Lord Jesus Christ; therefore, they are saved. *Acts 16:31*

♦ I confess that my children obey and respect their parents in all things. For this is pleasing unto the Lord. *Colossians 3:20*

♦ I confess that all of my children love the Lord with all of their heart, soul, strength, and might. *Deuteronomy 6:5*

♦ I confess that my children love, honor, and respect their father and mother. For this is the first commandment with promise. And with this promise, God promises them a long, healthy, and prosperous life. *Ephesians 6:2-3*

♦ As a parent, I shall not provoke my children to wrath or anger, but I shall teach them, and bring them up in the nurture and admonition of the Lord. *Ephesians 6:4*

♦ I confess that my children are faithful to keep the Word and ways of the Lord. Therefore, the promises and blessings of Abraham are upon my children. *Genesis 18:19*

♦ I confess that the Lord is with my children, and He prospers them in all they put their hands to do. *Genesis 39:3*

♦ I confess that my children have a hunger to hear the Word of God. And not only do they hear the Word of the Lord, they are also faithful and diligent to obey and follow the Word—thereby not deceiving themselves. *James 1:22*

♦ I confess that the Lord keeps my children from all evil. *John 17:15*

♦ I confess that the Lord is able to keep all of my children from falling, and to present them faultless before the presence of His glory with exceeding joy. Therefore, none of my children shall fall to drugs, alcohol, sexual sin, or sexual perversions; neither shall they fall to any ungodly addictions or strongholds of the enemy. *Jude 1:22*

♦ I confess that my children increase daily in wisdom and stature, and in the favor of God. And because they have favor with God, they have favor with all those who are in authority over them, as well as others around them. *Luke 2:52*

◆ I confess that my children have the mind of Christ Jesus. *Philippians 2:5*

◆ I confess that my God supplies all of the needs for all of my children according to His riches in glory by Christ Jesus. *Philippians 4:19*

◆ I confess that as I walk in integrity before my children as a parent, that my children shall also walk in integrity before the Lord, and shall be blessed by Him. *Proverbs 20:7*

◆ I confess that as I have taught and trained my children in the Word and ways of the Lord, as they grow older, they shall never be able to depart from the Lord, or depart from His ways or His Word. *Proverbs 22:6*

◆ I trust in the Lord with all of my heart concerning my children, and I do not lean to, or rely on my own understanding. As I acknowledge the Lord in all of my ways concerning my children, He directs my path. He instructs me how to teach them, and He leads and guides me in giving them direction and instruction in life. *Proverbs 3:5-6*

◆ I confess that my children do not walk or live under the influence or counsel of those who are ungodly; nor do they live, talk, or act like sinners. But I confess that my children have a joy and love for hearing the Word of God. I confess that they meditate and think upon the Word of God continually. And as a result, they are blessed and prosperous like a tree that is planted by the rivers of waters, which always bears good fruit. I decree (according to the Word of God) that none of the blessings of the Lord upon their lives shall ever wither or be taken away from them, and they shall prosper in whatever they do in life. *Psalms 1:1-3*

♦ I confess that as my children hear the Word of God, they also hide the Word of God deep within their hearts. And as a result, they shall not sin against the Lord. *Psalms 119:11*

♦ The Lord preserves my children from all evil; He preserves their soul. *Psalms 121:7*

♦ The Lord leads my children in truth, and teaches them to do what is right. For He is the God of their salvation. *Psalms 25:5*

♦ The Lord is the Shepherd and the provider of my children. Therefore, they shall not want or lack for any good, beneficial, or needful thing in their lives. The Lord causes my children to lie down in the green pastures of His blessings of abundance. He keeps their minds in peace. He restores and strengthens them when they need help. He leads them in the paths of His righteousness for His namesake. Whenever they go through dangers, tests, and trials, they will not walk in fear, because they know that the Lord is with them, and His Spirit and His Word comfort them. His anointing and presence is upon them, and even runs over. Surely, the goodness and mercy of the Lord shall follow each of my children all the days of their lives, and they shall dwell in the presence of the Lord forever. *Psalms Chapter 23*

♦ I confess that my children dwell in the secret place of the Most High God, and they abide under His almighty shadow of protection. I say of the Lord, that He is their refuge, defense, and place of protection. And it's in Him that they place their trust.

The Lord shall surely deliver my children from every snare and trap of the devil. He shall also deliver them from every sickness or disease that comes against their body.

He shall cover them with His feathers of protection, and under His wings of safety shall they put their trust. The truth of God's Word shall shield them and hold them together. They shall not be afraid of terror or danger (seen or unseen). They shall not be fearful or afraid of deadly diseases or destruction of any kind. Even though they may see many fall victim to different calamities and afflictions all around them, none of these calamities or afflictions shall come upon, or even near my children, because they have made the Lord their dwelling place and habitation.

No evil shall be able to come upon them, and no sickness or disease can even come near them. God has given His angels a command to watch over, protect, and guard my children. They are encamped in a continual hedge around them—protecting them from all hurt, harm, and danger. My children walk in the authority of Christ, and they therefore tread over all the powers of Satan.

Because my children love the Lord, the Lord shall keep them out of harms way, and deliver them from every adverse situation against them. When my children are in trouble and they call upon the Lord for help, He shall answer them, deliver them, and honor them.

The Lord shall bless my children with a long, happy, healthy, safe, and prosperous life, as He continually shows them His salvation. *Psalms Chapter 91*

Confessions
For Single Christians

♦ As a single Christian, I belong to the Lord. My heart and my soul belongs to Him. All that I am, and all that I have belongs to Him. My focus and passion are continually upon Him, loving Him, serving Him, and how I may please Him. *1 Corinthians 7:32, 34*

♦ I keep my heart as a virgin unto the Lord, and I stand steadfast (in my heart) in my love and my commitment unto Him. *1 Corinthians 7:37*

♦ As a singe Christian, I am mature in Christ. I am strengthened, established, and fully settled in Him. *1 Peter 5:10*

♦ The Lord is my comforter and my companion. Whenever I am lonely, He speaks to my heart, keeps me company, and comforts me. *John 14:16,26*

♦ As a single Christian, I am purged unto the Lord. I am a vessel of honor unto Him. I am sanctified, set aside, available for His use, and prepared for His good work. *1 Timothy 2:21*

♦ I flee youthful lusts, and I follow righteousness, faith, love, and the peace of God out of a pure heart. *2 Timothy 2:22*

♦ I walk in one accord with Christ, and I stay in continual fellowship with Him. For He is my hope, my purpose, and my singleness of heart. *Acts 2:46*

♦ As a single Christian, I walk virtuously unto the

Lord at all times—pleasing Him in all my ways and my works, and constantly increasing in the knowledge of His will. *Colossians 1:10*

♦ Even though I am single, I am complete in Christ. For He is my head and my companion. *Colossians 2:10*

♦ I love the Lord with all my heart, all my soul, all my strength, and all my might. For He is the lover of my soul. *Deuteronomy 6:5*

♦ I am rooted, grounded, settled, and established in my love for Christ, and in my relationship with Him. *Ephesians 3:17*

♦ I do not keep company or fellowship with those who would influence me to sin against God, do wrong, or commit evil. For I will not give any place to the devil in my life. *1 Corinthians 5:11 & Ephesians 4:27*

♦ I am crucified with Christ; nevertheless I live; yet it's not I that live, but Christ that lives in me. And the life that I now live as a single Christian, I live it by the faith, power, strength, and comfort of the Son of God, who loves me, and gave His life for me. *Galatians 2:20*

♦ The Lord comforts me and keeps me in His perfect peace, as I keep my heart and mind fastened and stayed upon Him. *Isaiah 26:3*

♦ I know the voice of the Lord, and I will only follow His voice. I will not be seduced or deceived in following the voice and seduction of the stranger (Satan), but I will follow the voice of my good shepherd, Jesus Christ. *John 10:5*

♦ The Lord leads me, guides me, and teaches me all things by the Comforter—the Holy Ghost that is within me. *John 14:26*

♦ The Lord is well able, and He will keep me from falling to the sins and seductions of the flesh. *Jude 1:24*

♦ As a single Christian, I keep watch and I pray; therefore, the enemy cannot enter into my life to deceive me, or lure me into sin or seduction. *Matthew 26:41*

♦ I am strong in the Lord and in the power of His might. I put on, and keep on the whole armor God. I am therefore able to stand against all the temptations and deceptions of the enemy. *Ephesians 6:10-11*

♦ It is my joy in the Lord (in fellowshipping with Him, serving Him, and dwelling with Him) that gives me the strength to live a victorious life as a single Christian. *Nehemiah 8:10*

♦ The Lord is a friend to me, and He loves and comforts me at all times. For He is a friend that sticks closer than any brother. *Proverbs 17:17 & Proverbs 18:24*

♦ The Lord is my shepherd, and He supplies all of my needs, wants, and desires. *Psalms 23:1*

♦ My delight as a single Christian is in the Lord; therefore, He blesses me and gives me the desires of my heart. *Psalms 37:4*

♦ The Lord delivers me from every trap and snare of the enemy. *Psalms 91:3*

♦ I am not conformed to the world's view of being single. Instead, my heart and mind are transformed daily to the image of Christ as a single Christian, because I constantly renew my mind in the Word of God. *Romans 12:2*

Confessions
For Protection and Safety

♦ God is my rock. It's in Him that I put my trust to protect and keep me. He is my shield from danger, and the source of my salvation. He is also my high tower, my refuge, and my Savior. *2 Samuel 22:3*

♦ The Lord is faithful unto me. He has established me in safety, and He keeps me from all evil. *2 Thessalonians 3:3*

♦ I know in whom I have believed—the Lord God strong and mighty. For I am fully persuaded that He is able to keep me from all evil and danger. *2 Timothy 1:12*

♦ The Lord shall keep me, and deliver me from every evil work and attack against me. He will preserve me unto His heavenly kingdom, to whom be glory forever and ever. *2 Timothy 4:18*

♦ The Lord shall cause my enemies (demon spirits that come against me) to be smitten and defeated before my face. They shall come out against me one way, but because of the glory and anointing of the Lord that is upon me, they shall be forced to flee from before me seven different ways. *Deuteronomy 28:7*

♦ I confess and boldly say that the Lord is my helper, and I will not fear what any man can do unto me. *Hebrews 13:6*

♦ God is my salvation. I will trust in Him, and I will not be afraid. For the Lord *Jehovah* is my strength and my protector. He alone is my salvation. *Isaiah 12:2*

♦ No weapon that is formed against my family or me shall be able to prosper in any way. And the Lord shall condemn the words of every person who talks or speaks against us. For this is my heritage as a servant of the Lord, and my righteousness is of Him. *Isaiah 54:17*

♦ God is able to keep me from falling victim to any evil or danger, and to present me faultless and without harm. *Jude 1:24*

♦ The name of the Lord is a strong tower. The righteous run to it, and they are safe. I am the righteousness of God, and I am safe in the name of the Lord. *Proverbs 18:10*

♦ I am the apple of God's eyes, and He hides me and keeps me safe under the shadow of His wings. *Psalms 17:8*

♦ The Lord is my light and my salvation; therefore, I have no need to fear. The Lord is the strength of my life; therefore, I shall not be afraid. *Psalms 27:1*

♦ Though many may come against me, my heart shall not fear. And though a multitude rise up against me, in this will I be confident: That the Lord is my light and my salvation. *Psalms 27:3*

♦ The Lord is my shield and my protection, and He is the lifter of my head. *Psalms 3:3*

♦ The Lord sustains me, and He will never allow my feet to be moved. *Psalms 55:22*

♦ The Lord is my shelter and my strong tower from my enemies. *Psalms 61:3*

♦ None of my enemies (spiritual or physical) shall be able to prosper against me, and neither shall they be able to afflict me in any way. *Psalms 89:22*

♦ My God is for me and with me. And, since He is, no person, spirit, or power is strong enough or able to come against me and succeed in any way. *Romans 8:31*

♦ I dwell in the secret place of the Most High God, and I abide under the shadow of His protection. *Psalms 91:1*

♦ The Lord is my refuge and my fortress; I place my trust in Him. *Psalms 91:2*

♦ Because I dwell in the secret place of the Most High, no evil shall be able to come upon me, and no plague or sickness can come near me. *Psalms 91:10*

♦ God has given His angels a charge (a command) to keep watch over me, and keep me in all of my ways— spiritually and physically. They stand guard in a vigilant hedge of protection around me, so that no accidents, hurt, harm, or danger can come upon me. *Psalms 91:12*

♦ Because I have set my love upon the Lord, He shall deliver me from all evil and danger. He has set me upon high (out of harm's way), because I have intimately known His name. *Psalms 91:14*

Confessions
For When You are Fearful or Afraid

♦ The Lord goes before me. He is always with me. He will never fail to protect me, and neither shall He ever forsake me. Therefore, I will not fear, nor be dismayed. *Deuteronomy 31:8*

♦ When I come upon dangerous situations and circumstances, the Lord shall be with me. When I go through fiery trials of affliction, I shall not be burned (injured or harmed), and neither shall any trace or effect of the trial or affliction be found upon me. *Isaiah 43:2*

♦ The Lord is my confidence. He keeps me from being fearful, and from being moved. *Proverbs 3:26*

♦ I dwell in the perfect love of God. Therefore, I will not be tormented with fear. For the perfect love of God casts out all fear. *I John 4:18*

♦ I am born of God; therefore, I overcome fear. For it is through my faith that God gives me victory to overcome the fears of the world. *I John 5:4*

♦ God has not given me a spirit of fear. Instead, He has given me a spirit of power, and of love, and a sound and peaceful mind. *II Timothy 1:7*

♦ The Lord is my help and my defense; therefore, I will not fear what any person, force, or spirit can do to me. *Hebrews 13:6*

♦ I will not walk in fear, because the Lord is with me. I

will not be afraid, because the Lord strengthens and helps me. He will always protect me, and He will always uphold me with the right hand of His righteousness. *Isaiah 41:10*

♦ The Lord contends (fight on my behalf) with every person, force, or spirit that comes against me. *Isaiah 49:25*

♦ No weapon that is formed against me—spiritually, physically, or by any other means shall be able to prosper against me. And every word that is spoken against me shall fall to the ground. For this is my heritage as a servant of the Lord. *Isaiah 54:17*

♦ The Lord has given me His peace. His peace is upon me. His peace is not the (conditional or circumstantial) peace of this world, but rather, the true, inner peace and comfort of God. Therefore, my heart shall not be troubled, and neither shall I be afraid. *John 14:27*

♦ The peace of God that passes all of man's understanding shall keep my heart and mind through Jesus Christ. *Philippians 4:7*

♦ The Lord redeems and protects my life from every attack against me, and He crowns me with His loving kindness and tender mercies. *Psalms 103:4*

♦ Since the Lord is on my side, I will not fear what any man can do unto me. *Psalms 118:6*

♦ The Spirit of the Lord always goes before me to protect me, keep me, and guard me. Therefore, I shall not be moved. *Psalms 16:8*

♦ Even when I go through dangers and afflictions, I will fear no evil, for the Lord is with me. His Word and His Spirit shall comfort me. *Psalms 23:4*

♦ Since the Lord is my light and my salvation, I shall

not be fearful. And, since the Lord is the strength of my life, I shall not be afraid. *Psalms 27:1*

♦ When people come against me, my heart shall not fear. When violence and danger is all around me, I will not be afraid. For in this I will still be confident: that the Lord is my light and my salvation. *Psalms 27:3*

♦ In times of trouble, the Lord hides me in the secret place of His tabernacle, and He sets me safe upon a rock out of harm's way. *Psalms 27:5*

♦ The Lord is my hiding place. He preserves me from trouble, and He surrounds me with His protection and deliverance. *Psalms 32:7*

♦ The angels of the Lord are encamped in a hedge of protection around me, because I reverence and fear the Lord. *Psalms 34:7*

♦ I dwell in the secret place of the Most High God, and I abide under the almighty shadow of His protection. The Lord is my place of refuge and my defense. He alone is the God in whom I put my trust. *Psalms 91:1-2*

♦ Because I dwell in the secret place of God, I shall not be afraid of any terror or dangers—seen or unseen. *Psalms 91:5-6*

♦ Since God is with me and for me, then no person, power, or force can prosper or succeed against me. *Romans 8:41*

Confessions For Your Faith

♦ Jesus Christ has given me His strength, His power, and His authority. Therefore, I can do all things through Christ who strengthens me. *Philippians 4:13*

♦ I am a person of faith; therefore, I do not look upon or focus upon the things that are seen, but my focus and attention are upon the things that are unseen in the spiritual realm. For the things that are seen are temporary and subject to change (to the Word of God that I speak). And, the things that are not seen are eternal, and shall stand forevermore. *2 Corinthians 4:18*

♦ I am a person of faith. I walk by faith; I talk by faith; I live by faith, and I therefore have an expectancy to receive that which I confess and pray for by faith. For I walk by faith and not by sight. *2 Corinthians 5:7*

♦ I am grounded in my faith in Christ Jesus and the Word of God. I am also rooted and settled in my faith, and I shall not be moved away from the hope of the gospel that I speak and believe. *Colossians 1:23*

♦ I am rooted and built up in Christ Jesus. I am established in my faith in the Word of God, and I abide therein with thanksgiving. *Colossians 2:7*

♦I gird myself daily with the shield of faith. I have faith in God. I have faith in God's Word, and I have faith in the authority that God has given unto me to decree and declare His Word. And with my faith, I quench all the fiery darts of the wicked one. *Ephesians 6:16*

♦ I hold fast to the confession of my faith (in God and in His Word). I do not waiver in my faith. I do not doubt, and I will not give up. For Christ is faithful who promised His Word. *Hebrews 10:23*

♦ My faith is "now faith." When I speak in faith, I believe that I have received it "now." For my faith is the substance of things hoped for, and the evidence of things not yet seen. *Hebrews 11:1*

♦ Without faith, it is impossible to please the Lord. But I please the Lord with my faith. For when I come to God, I believe that He is God, and God alone, and He is a rewarder of those that come unto Him and diligently seek His face. *Hebrews 11:6*

♦ Jesus Christ is the author and finisher of my faith, who, for the joy that was set before Him, endured the cross, despising shame, and is set down at the right hand of the throne of God. *Hebrews 12:2*

♦ For unto us (those who have heard, believed, and received the Word of God) was the gospel preached, as well as unto others who did not believe and receive the Word. The Word does not profit some because they do not mix it with faith. But the Word does profit me, because I mix the Word of God with my faith; therefore, when I release my faith in that which I believe and speak, those things shall profit me and shall come to pass. *Hebrews 4:2*

♦ When I pray and ask the Lord for something, I ask in faith. I do not waiver, and nor am I double minded; therefore, I receive that which I ask of God. *James 1:6*

♦ I build up myself daily in my faith, by diligently praying in the Holy Ghost. *Jude 1:20*

♦ I have mountain-moving faith that removes all hindrances and spiritual opposition. Therefore, when I command any mountains to be removed, they must move from before me. For with my faith (in God), nothing is impossible unto me. *Matthew 17:20*

♦ Because I walk in faith and do not doubt, I can do what Jesus did to the fig tree. I can speak to negative situations and circumstances in my life and command them to cease to exist, and they must obey me and cease. *Matthew 21:21*

♦ The righteousness of God is revealed from faith to faith. I am the just, and I live by faith. *Romans 1:17*

♦ My faith comes as a result of me reading, speaking, and hearing the Word of God. *Romans 10:17*

♦ As I speak the Word of God in faith, I call and confess those things which are not (according to the Word of God), as though they were (according to the Word of God), and they shall come to pass. *Romans 4:17*

♦ I will not stagger nor waiver at the promises of God through unbelief. But I will remain strong in my faith, giving glory to God. *Romans 4:20*

♦ I am fully persuaded in my heart and in my mind, that whatever God has promised me (according to His Word), He is well able to perform and bring to pass. *Romans 4:21*

♦ When my faith is tried in the fire, my faith shall stand and come through the fire victoriously—as pure gold. *1 Peter 1:7*

♦ I am sober in my faith, and I gird myself daily with the armor of faith. *1 Thessalonians 5:8*

Confessions
For Your Healing

♦ Jesus Christ bore my sins, sickness, and diseases on His own body upon the tree (cross). And with the stripes that He bore upon His body for me, I am healed. *1 Peter 2:24*

♦ The grace of the Lord is more than sufficient enough to heal my body. He causes my weakness to become strong, and He causes my infirmities to become healed. *2 Corinthians 12:9*

♦ I do not look at or focus on the things that are seen (the circumstances with my body). Instead, I choose to look at and focus my attention on the things that are not seen (my healing according to the Word of God). For the situation with my body is only temporary, and it is subject to change. But the spiritual things that I have spoken over my body (the Word of God) have been established by God, and shall come to pass. *2 Corinthians 4:18*

♦ The Lord has not given me a spirit of fear or doubt (concerning my healing), but He has given me a spirit of power, and of love, and a sound and confident mind that I shall receive my healing. *2 Timothy 1:7*

♦ It is God's desire for me above all things that I may prosper, and walk in whole and complete health in my body, mind, and emotions, even as I grow and prosper in the spirit. *3 John 1:2*

♦ I will not fear or doubt the Lord concerning my healing, but I will allow the peace of God to comfort my heart and my mind. *Colossians 3:15*

♦ It is the Lord that goes before me. He shall be with me; He shall not forsake me, and He shall not fail to heal my body. *Deuteronomy 31:8*

♦ The Lord shall remove all sickness and disease from my body. *Deuteronomy 7:15*

♦ The Lord shall not allow any disease or sickness to touch my body. *Exodus 15: 26*

♦ As I serve the Lord, He shall bless me, and He shall take sickness away from me. *Exodus 23:25*

♦ The Lord fulfills the number of my days; therefore, I shall live a long and full life. *Exodus 23:26*

♦ The Lord has commanded my body to rise, be healed, and to live. *Ezekiel 16:6*

♦ There is nothing too hard for the Lord. There is no disease or sickness too hard for the Lord to heal or deliver; therefore, by the grace and power of God, I receive my healing from the Lord. *Genesis 18:14*

♦ Jesus Christ is the same yesterday, today, and forever. And as the Lord has healed others, He is still the same God who is more than able and willing to heal my body. *Hebrews 13:8*

♦ The Lord gives me power when I am weak. And when I am sick, He heals my body and gives me strength. *Isaiah 40:29*

♦ Every valley shall be exalted, and every mountain and hill shall be made low. And every crooked thing (sickness or disease) that is in or upon my body shall be made straight, and I shall be healed. *Isaiah 40:4*

♦ The Lord shall contend with (rebuke and drive out) every sickness and disease that contends with (comes against) my body. *Isaiah 49:25*

♦ Jesus Christ has bore our grief and carried our sorrows. He has been stricken and smitten of God for my afflictions. For He was wounded for my transgressions; He was bruised for my iniquities; the chastisement of my peace was upon Him, and with His stripes, I am healed. *Isaiah 53:4-5*

♦ No weapon of sickness or disease that is formed against my body shall prosper. *Isaiah 54:17*

♦ Through the power of the Holy Ghost, God has anointed me to loose the bands of wickedness, to undo heavy burdens, to let the oppressed go free, and to break every yoke. Therefore, in the name of Jesus Christ, I break this yoke of sickness from my body. *Isaiah 58:6*

♦ As I continue to pray and confess the Word of the Lord concerning my healing, my light shall break forth in the morning, and my health shall spring forth speedily, as the righteousness of God goes before me. *Isaiah 58:8*

♦ As I humble myself in the sight of the Lord, He shall lift me up (from the place of sickness and disease), and restore me to good health. *James 4:10*

♦ Whenever there is sickness or disease upon me, I can call for the elders (mature men and women of prayer) to join with me in prayer, and anoint me with oil in the name of the Lord. And the prayer of faith that is made on my behalf, delivers me from sickness and disease, and restores me to good health. *James 5:14-15*

♦ As I have prayed for others to be healed, the Lord is faithful to also heal my body when I pray. For the effectual fervent prayers of a righteous man or women of God avails much. *James 5:16*

♦ Since the Lord has declared for me to be healed, I shall be healed. And since He has declared for me to be saved, I shall be saved and delivered. Therefore, my praise belongs to the Lord. *Jeremiah 17:14*

♦ The Lord shall restore health unto me, and He shall heal my infirmities. *Jeremiah 30:17*

♦ The Lord gives me good health. He cures all of my sickness and diseases, and gives me peace. *Jeremiah 33:6*

♦ As a king unto the most High King, Jesus Christ, I decree my healing to be established. *Job 22:28*

♦ As a king, unto the Most High King, Jesus Christ, I speak to every molecule, cell, tissue, organ, system, and every part of my body, and I command you to fall in line, and function correctly in the order in which God created you to function and perform. Job *22:28, Ecclesiastes 8:4, Matthew 21:21*

♦ As I pray and confess the Word of God over my body, my health shall be restored and renewed like that of a child. *Job 33:25*

♦ The thief comes to steal, kill, and destroy. But Jesus Christ has come to not only give me eternal life, but to also give me the abundant life of success, prosperity, and good health. *John 10:10*

♦ As I have prayed and asked the Lord for healing, I shall receive my healing—that my joy may be full. *John 16:24*

♦ As I speak the Word of God concerning my healing, the virtue of the Lord comes upon me and heals me. *Luke 6:19*

♦ The Lord has rebuked the devourer for my sake; therefore, Satan cannot destroy my health, and neither can He bring any sickness or disease upon me. *Malachi 3:11*

♦ Because I reverence the name of the Lord, He shall arise unto me with healing in His wings, and I shall go forth and prosper in good health. *Malachi 4:2*

♦ God has given me power and authority to speak to my mountains. So by the authority that He has given unto me through Christ Jesus, I command every sickness, disease, and spirit of infirmity to be removed from my body and cast into the sea. I do not doubt the Word of God concerning my healing. I believe that I have already received it. Therefore, I shall have what I have spoken. *Mark 11:23-24*

♦ I am a believer, and these signs follow me: In the name of Jesus Christ I cast out devils; I speak with new tongues; I lay hands upon the sick, and they do recover. I have the authority (through Christ) to not only lay hands upon others, but to also lay hands upon my own body. I therefore lay my hands upon my body, and I decree and declare that I am healed by the stripes of Jesus Christ. *Mark 16:17*

♦ Jesus has declared that healing is the children's (children of God) bread. I am a child of God. Therefore, healing belongs to me, and I receive my healing in the name of the Lord. *Matthew 15:26*

♦ As Jesus cursed the fig tree and told it to die—it died. Jesus has also given me the same authority; therefore, I curse this sickness and disease from my body, and I command it to die at the roots. And, as the fig tree ceased to live after Jesus cursed it, I decree that as I have cursed this sickness, that it shall also cease to dwell upon my body. *Matthew 21:19*

♦ The Word of God has been fulfilled which was spoken by the prophet Esaias, saying, Jesus Christ took my infirmities, and He bore my sickness and diseases upon the cross. *Matthew 8:17*

♦ I speak and declare the Word of God that this sickness shall not continue upon my body, nor shall it come upon me again. *Nahum 1:9*

♦ God is not a man that can lie; neither does He need to repent like man. Whatever the Lord has spoken concerning my healing, He shall do it; and for every promise He has made me concerning my healing, He shall make it good. *Numbers 3:19*

♦ I am confident in this very thing: That as the Lord has begun this good work of healing in my body, He is well able, and He will complete it. *Philippians 1:6*

♦ The peace of God that passes all of man's understanding shall keep my heart and mind through Jesus Christ as I go through this affliction. *Philippians 4:7*

♦ The tongue of the wise shall speak health; therefore, I speak healing and good health unto my body. *Proverbs 12:8*

♦ The Lord is far from the wicked, but He hears the prayers of the righteous when they call unto Him. And as I call unto Him concerning my healing, He hears and answers my prayers. *Proverbs 15:29*

♦ The Spirit of God shall sustain me and heal me of my infirmities. *Proverbs 18:14*

♦ The Word of God is health unto my body, and marrow to my bones. *Proverbs 3:8*

♦ I will give close attention to the Word of God, and I listen carefully to what He says. I will not let His Word depart from my eyes, and I will keep it in the midst of my heart. For the Word of God brings life unto my soul, and health unto my body. *Proverbs 4:20-22*

♦ I will bless the Lord from the depths of my soul. And with all that is within me, I will bless His holy name, and give Him thanksgiving and praise for His marvelous benefits: For He forgives all of my iniquities; He heals all of my sickness and diseases; He redeems my life and my body from every destruction and attack of the enemy; He crowns me with loving kindness and tender mercies; He gives me good things; and He renews my life, health, and strength like He does the eagle. *Psalms 103:2-5*

♦ The Lord has sent His Word unto me, and He has healed and delivered me from every affliction. *Psalms 107:20*

♦ The Lord's blessings and mercies are upon me to be healed; therefore, I shall not die, but I shall live and declare the mighty works of the Lord. *Psalms 118:17*

♦ My comfort in my affliction is this: The Word of the Lord has healed me. *Psalms 119:50*

♦ I will lift up my eyes unto the Lord who is the source of my help (and my healing). For my help comes from the Lord who made heaven and earth. *Psalms 121:1-2*

♦ The Lord will perfect (take care of, deliver me from,

and heal me of) the things that concern me. And since this sickness concerns me, the Lord shall heal and deliver me. For the mercy of the Lord endures forever. *Psalms 138:8*

♦ When I am sick, the Lord shall raise me up. For the Lord loves the righteous. *Psalms 146:8*

♦ It is the Lord who restores my soul and my body, and He leads me in the paths of righteousness for His name-sake. Even when I walk through the valley and the shadow of affliction, I will fear no evil, for the Lord is with me; His Word and His spirit comforts me. *Psalms 23:3-4*

♦ As I wait upon the Lord, I will be of good courage, for He shall strengthen and heal me. *Psalms 27:14*

♦ The Lord is my God; when I cry unto Him concern-ing my affliction, He shall heal me. *Psalms 30:2*

♦ I am of good courage, because I have faith that the Lord shall strengthen me in my affliction. *Psalms 31:24*

♦ Many are the afflictions of the righteous, but the Lord shall deliver me from out of them all. *Psalms 34:19*

♦ As I cast this burden of sickness upon the Lord, He shall sustain me with good health. *Psalms 55:22*

♦ God is my healer, and the strength of my heart, and my portion forever. *Psalms 73:26*

♦ No evil shall come upon me, and no sickness or dis-ease can come near my body. *Psalms 91:10*

♦ When I call upon the Lord concerning my sickness and infirmities, He shall answer me. He will be with me in trouble. He will deliver me and honor me. He will satisfy me with a long, healthy, and blessed life, and continually show me His salvation. *Psalms 91:15-16*

♦ The Lord is not a respecter of persons. As He has healed others, He shall also heal me. *Romans 2:11*

♦ I am a man/woman of faith. I call those things that be not as though they were. Therefore, in the name of Jesus Christ, I confess that I am totally and completely healed, and I walk in good health. *Romans 4:17*

♦ I am fully persuaded that what the Lord has promised me in His Word concerning my healing, that He is also able to perform and bring to pass. *Romans 4:21*

♦ Since God is for me, there is no sickness or disease that can prosper against my body, and there is no spirit or force that can keep me from receiving my healing. *Romans 8:31*

Confessions Concerning Your Needs

♦ This is the confidence that I have in the Lord: That if I ask Him anything according to His will, then I know He hears me. And, since I know that He hears me (no matter what I ask), then I also know that I have received the request and petition that I have desired and asked of Him. *1 John 5:14-15*

♦ Whatever I shall ask of the Lord, I shall receive of Him, because I keep His commandments, and do those things that are pleasing in His sight. *1 John 3:22*

♦ The grace of the Lord is sufficient to meet all of my needs. For all of my lack and needs are made sufficient through Him. *2 Corinthians 12:9*

♦ I am not sufficient in myself, but my sufficiency (needs being met) is in the Lord. *2 Corinthians 3:5*

♦ I do not look at or focus on the natural, physical things that are seen. But my focus and attention is on the (spiritual) things (that I have spoken according to the Word of God), which are unseen. For the natural, physical things that are seen are temporary and subject to change. But the spiritual, unseen things of God's Word are eternal. *2 Corinthians 4:18*

♦ God makes all grace to abound towards me, so that I have all sufficiency in all things. And He blesses me to prosper in every good work. *2 Corinthians 9:8*

♦ It is the Lord's desire for my life above all things that I may have success, prosperity, and be in good health, even as I prosper and grow spiritually. *3 John 1:2*

♦ The Lord is able to do exceedingly, abundantly, and above all I can ask or think (concerning my needs), according to the power of the Holy Ghost that works in and through me. *Ephesians 3:20*

♦ As I pray and speak the Word of God concerning my needs, God's Word shall not return unto me void or unanswered, but it shall accomplish and bring to pass, that which I have prayed, spoken, and confessed according to His Word. *Isaiah 55:11*

♦ When I have a need in my life and I seek the face of God concerning my need, the Lord hastens (quickens) His Word on my behalf. *Jeremiah 1:12*

♦ God has sent His Son, Jesus Christ, so that I may not only have life (eternal life), but that I may also have the abundant life of His blessings here on earth. *John 10:10*

♦ God has anointed me, and He has given me dominion power and authority as a king to speak to my circumstances, and to decree and declare His blessings over my life. Therefore, I speak and declare that "Money Cometh to me, now," from the north, south, east and the west, in the name of Jesus Christ! *Isaiah 43:6, Ecclesiastes 8:4, Matthew 17:20*

♦ As I pray and confess the Word of God concerning my needs and desires, I believe (by faith) that I have already received them; therefore, by faith, I shall have them. *Mark 11:24*

♦ I have faith in God and in His Word concerning my needs; therefore, all things are possible unto me. *Mark 9:23*

◆ Whatever I ask of the Lord in prayer, and confess according to His Word, I believe; therefore, I shall receive. *Matthew 21:22*

◆ I seek first the Kingdom of God and all of His righteousness; therefore, the Lord blesses me with my needs, and the desires of my heart. *Matthew 6:33*

◆ The Lord supplies all of my needs according to His riches in glory by Christ Jesus. *Philippians 4:19*

◆ With prayers, supplication, and thanksgiving, I let my requests be made known unto the Lord, and He answers my prayers. *Philippians 4:6*

◆ I will lift up my eyes unto the hills (unto the Lord), who is the source of my help (concerning my needs). For my help comes from the Lord. *Psalms 121:1-2*

◆ The Lord is my Shepherd, and I shall not want or lack for any good or needful thing in my life. *Psalms 23:1*

◆ The Lord blesses me to lie down in the green pastures of His provisions, and He leads me beside the still waters. *Psalms 23:2*

◆ The Lord prepares a table of blessings and provisions before me, even in the presence of those who are against me. He anoints and blesses me to such a degree, that my cup (blessings) runs over. *Psalms 23:5*

◆ Even the rich lack for something. But as I seek the Lord and trust in Him, I shall not lack any good or needful thing in my life. *Psalms 34:10*

◆ The eyes of the Lord are upon the righteous, and His ears are open to their cry. And since I am the righteousness of God in Christ, He sees my need, hears my request, and answers my prayer. *Psalms 34:15*

♦ Many are the needs and afflictions of the righteous, but the Lord delivers them from them all. And since I am the righteousness of God in Christ, the Lord shall meet my needs and deliver me. *Psalms 34:19*

♦ I've been young, and now I'm older. Yet the Lord has never forsaken me or failed to meet my needs, and neither has He allowed me to be forced to beg for bread. *Psalms 37:25*

♦ I delight myself in the Lord, His ways, and His Word; therefore, He gives unto me the needs and desires of my heart. *Psalms 37:4*

♦ The Lord God is a sun and shield. The Lord will give grace and glory. And no good or needful thing will He withhold from me as I walk uprightly before Him. *Psalms 84:11*

♦ I am a man/woman of faith. And by faith, I call those things that are not (according to the Word of God), as though they were (according to the Word of God). Therefore, I confess that _____ is/are established and manifested in my life. *Romans 4:17*

♦ I am fully persuaded, that what the Lord has promised me concerning my needs, He is well able to perform and bring to pass. *Romans 4:21*

Confessions
of Prosperity

♦ This is the confidence that I have in the Lord: That if I ask Him anything according to His Word and His will, He hears me. And since I know that He hears me—no matter what I ask, then I know that I have received the petitions (needs and desires) that I have desired and asked of Him. *1 John 15:14*

♦ The eyes of the Lord are upon the righteous. And since I am the righteousness of God in Christ Jesus, then I know that His ears are open to my prayers and requests. *1 Peter 3:12*

♦ God's desire above all things for me is that I may prosper, have good success, and walk in good health, even as I grow and prosper spiritually. *3 John 1:2*

♦ As I follow and obey the Word of the Lord, He causes His blessings to come upon my life and overtake me. *Deuteronomy 28:2*

♦ I am blessed in the city, and blessed in the field (in business and at work). I am blessed when I come in my home, and blessed when I go out of my home. My spouse and children are blessed and prosperous in every area of their lives. I am blessed with success, increase, and promotions upon my job, in business, and in every area of my life. *Deuteronomy 28:3-6*

♦ The Lord has commanded the blessings of increase to be upon my storehouses (my checking accounts, savings accounts, and investments), and He has blessed me to prosper and have increase in all that I put my hand to do. *Deuteronomy 28:8*

♦ I am blessed to be the lender, and not the borrower. I am blessed to be the head in all things, and not the tail. I am blessed to be above only (in my finances, job, and business), and never beneath. *Deuteronomy 28:13-14*

♦ Because of the blessings of the Lord upon my life, people shall see that I am called by the name of the Lord, and the Lord shall make me prosperous and plenteous in all things. *Deuteronomy 28:10-11*

♦ The Lord blesses me with all spiritual blessings in heavenly places in Christ. *Ephesians 1:3*

♦ The Lord continually blesses me exceedingly, abundantly, and above all I can ask or think, according to the power of the Holy Ghost that works in and through me. *Ephesians 3:20*

♦ I am the seed of Abraham (through Jesus Christ), and heirs according to the promise; therefore, the promises and blessings of Abraham are upon my life and my family. *Galatians 3:14, 29*

♦ The Lord leads me, and gives me His wisdom, knowledge, and understanding, and teaches me how to profit and prosper in all things. *Isaiah 48:17*

♦ As I pray, speak, and confess the Word of God, the Lord hastens (speeds up) the performance of His Word upon my life. *Jeremiah 1:12*

♦ I know the thoughts that God has towards me: Thoughts of peace, and not of evil, and to bring me to a blessed, bright, and prosperous future. *Jeremiah 29:11*

♦ I confess the Word of God continually, and I do not

allow the Word of God to cease from coming forth from my mouth. I meditate upon His Word, and confess the Word of God day and night. I obey the Word of God that I speak and confess. Therefore, the Lord blesses me to prosper, and He gives me good success. *Joshua 1:8*

♦ I seek first the Kingdom of God (in my life) and all His righteousness. Therefore, the blessings of God and the desires of my heart are continually added unto me. *Matthew 6:33*

♦ God has anointed me, and He has given me dominion power and authority as a king to speak to my circumstances, and to decree and declare His blessings over my life. Therefore, I speak and declare that "Money Cometh to me, now," from the north, south, east and the west, in the name of Jesus Christ! *Isaiah 43:6, Ecclesiastes 8:4, Matthew 17:20*

♦ My God supplies all of my needs and desires, according to His riches in glory by Christ Jesus. *Philippians 4:19*

♦ Like a tree planted by the rivers of water, I am blessed and prosperous. I bring forth good fruit (good and favorable results) in every season (situation and circumstance of my life). None of my leaves (blessings of the Lord upon my life) shall ever wither, and whatever I do, I shall prosper in it. *Psalms 1:3*

♦ The lines (blessings of the Lord) fall unto me in pleasant places. For I have a godly heritage. *Psalms 16:6*

♦ It is a sure thing that the goodness and mercy of the Lord shall follow me all the days of my life, and I shall dwell in the presence of the Lord forever. *Psalms 23:6*

♦ The Lord is magnified, and takes pleasure as He

prospers (me) His servant. *Psalms 35:27*

♦ My trust is in the Lord; therefore, I shall do good, and I shall dwell in the land of plenty. *Psalms 37:3*

♦ My delight is continually in the Word of the Living God, and He gives me the desires of my heart. *Psalms 37:4*

♦ The Lord opens doors (of blessings, prosperity, and success upon my life) that no man can shut. *Revelations 3:8*

♦ The Lord has opened the windows of heaven upon my life, and He continually pours out His blessings of abundance upon me, so that I do not have room to contain them all. *Malachi 3:10*

♦ The Lord has rebuked the devourer for my sake; therefore, Satan cannot destroy my finances, nor can he destroy any of the blessings that God has given unto me. *Malachi 3:11*

♦ Because of the blessings of the Lord upon my life, people of all race, color, and nationality shall look upon me and call me blessed, and they shall also call me a delightsome land (prosperous and blessed). *Malachi 3:12*

Confessions Over Your Tithes and Offerings

♦ As I sow in tithes, offerings, and gifts of love, the Lord multiplies my seed back unto me, and He increases them unto me bountifully. *II Corinthians 9:10*

♦ Because I sow bountifully, the Lord blesses me to also receive bountifully. *II Corinthians 9:6*

♦ I have determined to give unto the Lord from my heart. I do not give grudgingly, and neither do I give out of obligation, or of a necessity. But I gladly, joyfully, and freely give, because I love the Lord and desire to please Him, and because the Lord loves a cheerful giver. *II Corinthians 9:7*

♦ When I give unto the Lord, He always gives back unto me. He returns it to me in a good measure, pressed down, shaken together, and running over. He causes people to give unto me from every direction. For with the same heart that I give, the Lord multiplies my seed, and returns it back unto me again in abundance. *Luke 6:38*

♦ As I bring my tithe and offering into the Lord's house, He makes sure that there are provisions in my house. And as I give unto Him, He proves Himself to me by opening the windows of heaven and pouring me out blessings in my life (spiritually, physically, and financially) to such a degree, that I barely have room enough to receive them all. *Malachi 3:10*

Confessions
For the Favor of the Lord

♦ I have God's grace upon my life. And because of His grace, He gives me His unmerited favor. *2 Peter 1:2*

♦ God has given unto me an excellent spirit. Therefore, I have God's favor upon my life in every situation and circumstance. *Daniel 6:3*

♦ I grow daily in the grace of God; therefore, His favor is upon my life, and He also blesses me to have favor with all men. *1 Samuel 2:26*

♦ I have grace and favor in the sight of the Lord, and God therefore gives me favor and preferential treatment above others. I have preferred treatment with job assignments, advancements, promotions, business, and in every area and aspect of my life. *Esther 2:17*

♦ I have the favor of Joseph upon my life. No matter where I go or what I do, I will always rise to the top, because I am favored by the Lord. *Genesis 39:21*

♦ Many seek promotions and advancements by their underhanded plots and schemes, but the Lord blesses me to prosper above them because of His favor upon me. *Proverbs 29:26*

♦ Surely, the goodness, mercy, and favor of the Lord shall follow me everywhere I go, and I shall dwell in His presence all the days of my life. *Psalms 23:6*

♦ God's righteousness and favor are upon me. For He is magnified, and He takes pleasure in prospering me, advancing me, and showing Himself strong on my behalf before the world. *Psalms 35:27*

♦ The Lord surrounds me with His favor, and His presence preserves me. *Job 10:12*

♦ The anger of the Lord endures only for a moment. But His favor is upon me all the days of my life. *Psalms 30:5*

♦ Because I keep the commandments and statutes of the Lord upon my heart, He gives me favor and understanding in His sight, and in the sight of all men. *Proverbs 3:4*

♦ The Lord blesses me with His righteousness, and He covers me with His favor. *Psalms 5:12*

♦ Because of God's goodness upon my life, He gives me His favor. *Proverbs 12:2*

♦ Since God's blessings and favor are upon my life, there is no one who is able to stop me or hinder me from receiving what God has for me. *Romans 8:31*

Confessions
of Your Salvation

♦ I have been bought with the price of the precious blood of Jesus Christ; therefore, I will glorify God in my body and in my spirit, which belong to the Lord. *I Corinthians 6:20*

♦ I have been redeemed from the penalty of hell. My redemption was not purchased with the corruptible things of silver or gold, but with the precious blood of Jesus Christ—the Lamb of God who is without sin or iniquity. *I Peter 1:18-19*

♦ I am a son of God. And it does not appear what I shall be. But I know when He appears, I shall be like Him; for I shall see Him as He is. *I John 3:2*

♦ I am saved: For I have come unto the knowledge of the truth of the Word of God concerning my salvation. *I Timothy 2:4*

♦ The Lord is not slack concerning His promise (of salvation), but long-suffering, merciful, and patient towards us. For He does not desire that any person would perish (and miss eternal life), but that all would come to repentance. I therefore confess that all of my family members and relatives come to repentance, and receive eternal salvation through Jesus Christ, our Lord. *II Peter 3:9*

♦ I am dead unto Christ; therefore, I shall live with Him forever. *II Timothy 2:11*

♦ I have redemption through the blood of Jesus Christ, and all of my sins, iniquities, and transgressions have been forgiven, according to the riches of His grace. *Ephesians 1:7*

♦ I was once dead in my trespasses and sins. But the Lord has quickened me (brought my spirit to life), and now my spirit lives unto Jesus Christ forevermore. *Ephesians 2:1*

♦ It is by the abundant mercies of God towards me that I am saved. I am not saved by any of my works; neither am I saved by any good or charitable deeds. I am saved only by the grace of God, through my faith in His Son, Jesus Christ—the wonderful gift of God. *Ephesians 2:8*

♦ Jesus Christ has saved me with His precious blood; therefore, my salvation has been finalized and sealed unto the day of redemption. *Ephesians 4:30*

♦ Jesus Christ has not only saved me with His precious blood, He is also able to save all those who come unto Him, because He makes intercessions for us. *Hebrews 7:25*

♦ I have confessed with my mouth that Jesus Christ is Lord. I have also believed upon Him and received Him into my heart; therefore, I am saved. For it was with my heart that I believed unto righteousness, and it was with my mouth that I made my confession unto my salvation. *Romans 10:9-10*

♦ I have been freely justified by the grace of God through the redemption that is in Christ Jesus. *Romans 3:24*

♦ God has declared me righteous through the faith and blood of Jesus Christ. For through repentance, and the remission of my sins, He has made me to be the righteousness of God. *Romans 3:25*

♦ It was through the sin of Adam that the judgment of God came upon all of mankind unto condemnation. But by the grace of God and the righteousness of Jesus Christ, I have been given the free gift of salvation and justification, that is available to all those who receive Him. *Romans 5:18-19*

♦ When I was ungodly (without God), Christ died for me that I would be saved. *Romans 5:6,8*

♦ The spirit of God bears witness with my spirit, that I am a child of God. *Romans 8:16*

♦ I am a child of God. I am an heir of God, and a joint-heir with Christ. And as I suffer with Him, I shall also be glorified with Him. *Romans 8:17*

♦ The law of the spirit of Christ Jesus has made and set me free from the law of sin and eternal damnation. *Romans 8:2*

♦ For what the law could not do, being that it was weak through the flesh, God sent His only begotten Son, Jesus Christ, in the likeness of sinful flesh, and condemned sin in the flesh on my behalf. *Romans 8:3*

♦ I am saved—not by works of righteousness, but according to the mercy of God. I have been washed by the blood of Jesus Christ, and regenerated by the renewing of the Holy Ghost. *Titus 3:5*

Confessions
Over Your Prayer Life

♦ I am a man/woman of prayer. I will pray without ceasing. I will pray upon every situation that comes upon me, and I will pray whenever the Holy Spirit prompts my heart to pray. *I Thessalonians 5:17*

♦ I will not sin against the Lord by ceasing or failing to pray for others. *I Samuel 12:23*

♦ I am not ashamed to pray. I will pray anywhere and anytime the Lord leads me, and I will not be ashamed to lift up holy hands unto Him. *I Timothy 2:8*

♦ I pray always with all prayer and supplication in the spirit, and I intercede with all perseverance and supplication for other saints. *Ephesians 6:18*

♦ I am an intercessor. When I hear of people who have fallen, and who have been overtaken by sin, I will pray and intercede for them. And through my prayers and intercession, they shall be restored and strengthened in the Lord. *Galatians 6:1*

♦ Because of the blood of Jesus Christ, I have the privilege and the right to come boldly before the throne of God in prayer, which is where I find grace, mercy, and help in times of need. *Hebrews 4:16*

♦ Because I am a man/woman of prayer, my prayers avail much in victory. For the effectual, fervent prayers of a righteous man/woman of God avails much. *James 5:16*

♦ I pray daily in the Holy Ghost. And as I pray in the

Holy Ghost, I build up myself in God, and in my faith in Him through Jesus Christ. *Jude 1:20*

♦ Because I am a person of prayer, I always pray, and never stop, faint, or give up on that in which I am praying and believing. *Luke 18:1*

♦ I am disciplined in prayer. Each day I rise early in the morning at my appointed time of prayer and spend quality and intimate time with the Lord. *Mark 1:35*

♦ I am a person of faith and prayer. Whatever things I pray for, I believe that I have already received them (when I pray for them); therefore, I shall have them. *Mark 11:24*

♦ I am a porter. I stand watch in prayer over my life, my family, my home, and my church. Therefore, Satan cannot touch these, or any other area of my life. *Matthew 26:41*

♦ Each day I enter into my closet (my special, quiet place of prayer) and talk to the Father alone. But as I am dedicated and disciplined to spend quality and intimate time in prayer talking to God alone, He answers my prayers and rewards me openly. *Matthew 6:6*

♦ I do not allow things to worry me, because I commit all things to prayer and supplication unto the Lord, making my requests known unto Him. *Philippians 4:6*

♦ I am disciplined to direct my voice in prayer unto the Lord early in the morning. This is the time that I have set aside and established to look up unto the Lord, and direct my prayers unto Him. *Psalms 5:3*

♦ I am a person of prayer. I not only pray unto the Lord in the morning, but I also pray at noon and in the evening. And when I pray, the Lord hears my voice and answers my prayers. *Psalms 55:17*

♦ When I go through tribulation and trouble in my life, I will wait upon the Lord and be patient with Him by staying constant and steadfast in prayer. *Romans 12:12*

♦ There are times when I do not know what to pray for. There are also situations and circumstances in my life for which I don't even know how to pray. But in times like these, I will pray in the spirit. And as I pray in the spirit (even though I don't understand what I'm saying), the Holy Ghost helps my inability and lack of knowledge and understanding, by interceding on my behalf, and properly petitioning the Father. *Romans 8:26*

Confessions to Keep Your Hunger For God

♦ I glory in the name of the Lord, and my heart continually seeks Him. *I Chronicles 16:10*

♦ My heart and my soul seek the face of the Lord. *I Chronicles 22:19*

♦ I am risen with Christ, and I seek those things that are above—how I may please Him. *Colossians 3:1-2*

♦ Because I seek the Lord with all of my heart, I find Him, and dwell in His presence. *Deuteronomy 4:29*

♦ I love the Lord with all of my heart, all of my soul, all of my strength, and all of my might, and I seek His face. *Deuteronomy 6:5*

♦ I rise daily and seek the face of the Lord early while He may be found, and I call upon Him while He is near. *Isaiah 55:6*

♦ Through my prayer, confession, worship, and the fellowship in God's Word, I draw near to Him, and He therefore draws near to me. *James 4:8*

♦ My heart and my soul hungers for the Lord; and therefore, I am filled. *Luke 6:21*

♦ My first priority and passion in life is to seek first the Kingdom of God and all of His righteousness (how I may love and please Him, and draw near to Him). And as a result of my heart and passion to please Him, He causes all of my needs, and the desires of my heart to be added unto me. *Matthew 6:33*

♦ My heart is fixed to seek the face of the Lord and His strength with all my heart. *Psalms 105:4*

♦ As my soul hungers for the Lord, He satisfies me with His goodness. *Psalms 107:9*

♦ My heart and my soul thirsts after the goodness and the presence of the Lord, as if I was in a dry and thirsty land where there was no water. *Psalms 143:6*

♦ My greatest and earnest desire of the Lord is that I may dwell in the house of the Lord all the days of my life, to behold the beauty of the Lord, and dwell in His presence. *Psalms 27:4*

♦ As the deer pant and thirst for water, so does my soul pant and thirst after the Lord my God. *Psalms 42:1*

♦ My soul desires to follow hard after the Lord with a burning passion. *Psalms 63:8*

♦ My soul longs to be in the presence of the Lord; my heart and my flesh cry out for the living God. *Psalms 84:2*

Confessions
For the Word of God

♦ As newborn babies desire milk, I desire and crave the sincere milk (nourishment) of the Word of God; therefore, I grow and mature in Him. *I Peter 2:2*

♦ I am a student of the Word of God, and I diligently study His Word daily to show myself approved unto Him. I am a workman in the Word of God, and I am therefore not ashamed, because I know how to rightfully divide and skillfully use the Word of truth. *II Timothy 2:15*

♦ My heart hungers for the Word of God. I study His Word daily, and I stand always ready to hear and receive the Word with readiness of mind. *Acts 17:11*

♦ I believe on the Lord Jesus Christ, and I fellowship in His Word continuously; therefore, I am His disciple indeed. *John 8:31*

♦ I will not allow the Word of God to cease from coming from my mouth. I will meditate upon the Word of God throughout the day, the evening, and at night. I will be watchful and observant to obey all that is written in the Word. For it is in the Word of God that I shall make my way prosperous, and it is also through the Word of God that I shall have good success. *Joshua 1:8*

♦ I do not live and exist solely by natural food alone, but my soul is nourished and fed by every Word that comes out of the mouth of God. *Luke 4:4*

♦ I take delight in hearing, reading, and studying the Word of God, and I meditate upon His Word day and night. *Psalms 1:2*

♦ The revelation of God's Word gives me understanding, and enlightens my mind. *Psalms 119:30*

♦ When my soul wants to be slothful to hear, read, or confess the Word, I will not give *in* to my soul, but I will press my way forward to hear, read, and confess the Word of God. *Luke 5:1*

♦ I am blessed of the Lord because I hear His Word and I keep His commandments. *Luke 11:28*

♦ As the Word of God increases in me, I become more and more obedient to obey and follow the Word. *Acts 6:7*

♦ The Word of the Lord grows in me continually, and it is multiplied in my heart and my mind. *Acts 2:24*

♦ The Word of the Lord is perfect. It converts and transforms my heart, my mind, and my soul. The commandments and instructions of the Lord are right. They are sure, and they give illumination to my eyes, and understanding to my mind. The respect, reverence, and godly fear of the Lord are genuine, pure, and clean. His judgments are true and righteous altogether. I desire the Word of the Lord more than riches and fine gold. For the Lord is sweeter than the honey in a honeycomb. *Psalms 19:7-10*

♦ I have great faith in God, which comes as a result of my continual hearing, studying, and speaking the Word of God. *Romans 10:17*

♦ I take the sword of the spirit, which is the Word of God, and I pray His Word always with all prayer and supplication in the spirit. *Ephesians 6:17*

♦ I am strong in the Lord, and I overcome the wicked

one, because the Word of God abides within me. *I John 2:14*

Confessions
For Direction and Guidance

♦ The Lord gives me an understanding heart to judge and discern between good and evil, right and wrong, and what His will is for my life. *I kings 3:9*

♦ When I seek the Lord for His wisdom and direction, He freely gives me His wisdom, knowledge, and direction in all things that pertain to life and godliness. *2 Peter 1:3*

♦ The Lord enlightens my darkness, for He lights my way. *II Samuel 22:29*

♦ The Lord gives me knowledge and understanding in all things. *II Timothy 2:7*

♦ The Lord causes my understanding to become enlightened in things that I do not know, do not understand, and in things I cannot foresee. *Ephesians 1:18*

♦ Whenever I am confused or unsure about which direction to take, the Lord shall give me His answer of peace, which points me in the right direction. *Genesis 41:16*

♦ The Lord knows the end result of a thing before it actually begins. He therefore orders my footsteps, and directs me in the path of His will, that brings me to His blessing and a favorable outcome. *Isaiah 46:10*

♦ Whenever I lack wisdom and understanding, I will ask God. For He liberally gives me His wisdom and understanding without restraint. *James 1:5*

♦ Whenever I call upon the Lord concerning directions

and instructions for my life, He answers me and shows me great and mighty things that I did not know, and could not foresee. *Jeremiah 33:3*

♦ I know the voice of my good Shepherd, Jesus Christ, and I will only follow His voice. Whenever the stranger (Satan) speaks to me, I will ignore him, and will only follow the voice of the Lord. *John 10:5*

♦ The comforter—which is the Holy Ghost, teaches me all things, and brings all things to my remembrance that the Lord has spoken unto me. *John 14:26*

♦ I have the spirit of truth within me. For He guides and leads me in all things, and points me in the right direction. *John 16:13*

♦ Whenever I do not know what to say, the Holy Spirit teaches me and tells me what to say. *Luke 12:12*

♦ The Lord gives wisdom unto my mouth in the midst of my adversities. *Luke 22:15*

♦ The Lord gives me discretion, and with His wisdom, He preserves and keeps me from making the wrong choices and decisions. *Proverbs 2:11*

♦ The Lord gives me wisdom, and out of His mouth He gives me knowledge and understanding. *Proverbs 2:6*

♦ I trust in the Lord with all my heart (for His directions and instructions), and I do not lean or rely on my own understanding. *Proverbs 3:5*

♦ In every situation and circumstance of my life that I acknowledge the Lord, He shall give me instructions and direct my path. *Proverbs 3:6*

♦ In times of darkness and indecision, the Word of the

Lord is a lamp unto my feet, and a light unto my pathway. *Psalms 119:105*

♦ Because I trust in the Lord, He leads me in the way that I should go. *Psalms 143:8*

♦ I will bless the Lord, who gives counsel and instructions in my seasons of indiscretion. *Psalms 16:7*

♦ The Lord gives illumination to my mind, and He brightens my thoughts in times of darkness and confusion. *Psalms 18:28*

♦ The Lord leads me like a Shepherd, and supplies all my needs. And with His peace, He leads me and directs me in the path of His righteousness for His namesake. *Psalms 23:1-3*

♦ The Lord is my rock and my fortress. And for His namesake, He leads and guides me. *Psalms 31:3*

♦ The Lord instructs me and leads me in the way I am to go, and He guides me with His eyes continually. *Psalms 32:8*

♦ The Lord orders and directs the steps that I take, and He takes delight in guiding me in His ways. *Psalms 37:23*

♦ Because I am a son of God, I am lead by the Spirit of God. *Romans 8:14*

Confessions Over Anger

♦ I am of born of God. Through Christ, I have overcome the world, and I am therefore able to overcome anger. For greater is He (Jesus Christ) who is in me (who gives me power over the spirit of anger), than the enemy that is in the world. *1 John 4:4*

♦ Whenever I am approached in anger, or enticed to anger by others, I will not give in to, nor react in anger. Instead, I will respond in the wisdom, judgment, and peace of God. *1 Peter 2:23*

♦ God has not given me a spirit of fear (or anger), but He has given unto me a spirit of power (over anger), love, and a sound and peaceful mind. *2 Timothy 1:7*

♦ I have put off the old man, and I have now put on the new man, which is renewed in the image of Christ; therefore, I put off anger, malice, wrath, and all ungodly and unrighteous communication. *Colossians 3:8,10*

♦ Whenever I am tempted with anger, through the power of the Holy Ghost, I will not sin by giving *in* to anger. For I will not give the devil any place in my life. *Ephesians 4:26-27*

♦ I stand firm in my liberty in which Christ has set me free, and I will not be entangled again with the bondage and stronghold of anger. *Galatians 5:1*

♦ I am born of the spirit of God, and I am filled with His Spirit. I therefore possess and walk in the fruit of the spirit. I walk in love, joy, peace, longsuffering, gentleness, goodness, faith, meekness, and temperance. *Galatians 5:22-23*

♦ I confess according to the Word of God that I am swift to hear (willing to listen). I carefully consider what I say, and the attitude in which I say it. And I am therefore slow to become aroused or enticed to anger or wrath. *James 1:19*

♦ When people approach me with anger, rage, or indignation, I will respond with a soft and peaceful response. And, my response shall turn away their anger. *Proverbs 15:1*

Confessions Concerning Trouble In Your Life

The following are scripture confessions that can be used in a variety of ways. They can be used for confessions when you experience trouble, such as legal trouble or having trouble upon your job. They can also be used generally, such as having trouble in your marriage, family, with your children, finances, or any other means.

♦ God is my refuge and my strength. He is a very present help in times of trouble in my life. *Psalms 46:1*

♦ There is no trial that can come upon me, but such as those that have come upon others. But God is faithful, who will not allow me to go through any trouble or affliction unless He knows that I am able to bear it. And, when I must go through trouble or affliction, He will sustain me, and make a way of escape for me by taking me through my trouble in the comfort and peace of His Spirit. *1 Corinthians 10:13*

♦ I will not need to fight this battle alone. For the Lord shall fight for me. In this battle I shall stand still and see the salvation (deliverance) of the Lord. *2 Chronicles 20:17*

♦ When it looks like I'm troubled on every side, I know that I'm not in distress. When it seems that I'm perplexed, I know that I'm not in despair. When persecution comes upon me, I know that I have not been forsaken. And even when it looks like I'm cast down, I know that I'm not destroyed (because the Lord is with me). *2 Corinthians 4:8*

♦ I shall not fear, for the Lord is with me. I shall not worry or let my heart be troubled, for the Lord is my God. He will strengthen me and help me through this trouble, and He will uphold me with the right hand of His righteousness. *Isaiah 41:10*

♦ When I pass through troublesome waters and rivers of life, they shall not overflow me. When I go through fiery trials and afflictions, I shall not be burned, and neither shall the effects of the fire or storm consume me. There shall not even be a trace of the fire or storm upon me, because the Lord shall be with me in the midst of my storm and trouble. *Isaiah 43:2*

♦ I know the thoughts that the Lord has towards me concerning my troubles. They are thoughts of peace, victory, and deliverance—and not of evil. For He shall bring me through. *Jeremiah 29:11*

♦ My heart shall not be troubled or overwhelmed. For I believe in God, and in Jesus Christ, His Son. *John 14:1*

♦ I have the peace of God through Jesus Christ. My peace is not the world's kind of peace that is circumstantial and conditional. My peace is true, inner peace that comes from God. Therefore, my heart shall not be troubled or overwhelmed, and I shall not be afraid. *John 14:27*

♦ When I am in the midst of trouble, I shall allow the peace of God that passes all of man's understanding to keep my heart and mind through Jesus Christ. *Philippians 4:7*

♦ The name of the Lord is a strong tower for me (in the midst of trouble). I am the righteous, and as I draw near to Him, He comforts me and keeps me safe. *Proverbs 18:10*

♦ In the midst of my trouble, I will trust in the Lord with all of my heart. I will not lean to, or rely on my own understanding; but in all of my ways I will acknowledge Him, and He shall direct my path. *Proverbs 3:5-6*

♦ The Lord will not hide His face from me in the day when I am in trouble. He shall hear me, and He shall deliver me speedily in the day when I call upon His name. *Psalms 102:2*

♦ When I pray, confess the Word of the Lord, and cry unto Him in the midst of my trouble, He shall deliver me out of my distress. *Psalms 107:6*

♦ The Lord is on my side; therefore, I shall not fear what any man can do to me. *Psalms 118:6*

♦ I will lift up my eyes unto the Lord who is the source of my help and my deliverance. For my help comes from the Lord. He shall not allow me to be moved. For the Lord is my keeper. He is my protector and my deliverer. Therefore, I shall not be overcome or destroyed in the midst of this trouble. The Lord shall preserve me from all evil and destruction. He shall preserve my heart and my mind with His peace. He shall preserve my going out and my coming in from this time forth, and even forevermore. *Psalms 121:1-8*

♦ When I am in the midst of trouble, the Lord is with me, and His right hand saves and delivers me. *Psalms 138:7*

♦ The Lord shall hide me in the shelter of His secret place. He shall set me upon a rock, and deliver me from the midst of trouble. *Psalms 27:5*

♦ The Lord is my strength and my shield. When I trust in the Lord, He helps me. Therefore, my heart shall be at peace and shall rejoice, and I shall praise Him for my deliverance. *Psalms 28:7*

♦ The Lord makes His face to shine upon me, and He saves and delivers me out of trouble for His mercy's sake. *Psalms 31:16*

♦ The Lord is my hiding place. He shall preserve me from the effects of the storm. While I am in the storm, the Lord shall surround me with His presence and His joy, as He gives me deliverance. *Psalms 32:7*

♦ Many are the afflictions of the righteous, but the Lord delivers them from them all. And, since I am the righteousness of God in Christ, the Lord shall also deliver me from my afflictions. *Psalms 34:19*

♦ As I wait patiently for the Lord in the midst of my trouble, He shall listen unto me, hear my cry, and deliver me. *Psalms 40:1*

♦ The Lord shall bring me up and out of the miry clay (out of the midst of this trouble). He shall set my feet safe upon a rock (give me deliverance), and He shall establish my direction. *Psalms 40:2*

♦ Because I have set my love upon the Lord, He shall therefore deliver me out of trouble. He shall set me upon high, because I have intimately known His name. *Psalms 91:14*

♦ When I am in trouble, I can call upon the Lord, and He will answer me. For He shall be with me in trouble; He will deliver me and honor me. *Psalms 91:15*

♦ Whenever I call upon the name of the Lord in times of trouble, the Lord shall save me. *Romans 10:13*

♦ Even in times of trouble, the Lord shall cause all

things to work together for my good, because I love the Lord, and I am called according to His purpose. *Romans 8:28*

♦ Since God is for me (even in the midst of trouble), there is no person, spirit, or force that is strong enough or able to come against me and succeed. *Romans 8:31*

Confessions For Victory Over Sin, Strongholds, and Addictions

♦ There is no temptation that can come upon me, but those that have come upon others. But God is faithful, who will not allow me to be tempted above that which I am able to stand. And with every temptation that comes upon me, He will strengthen me, empower me, and enable me to overcome and escape the temptation. *I Corinthians 10:13*

♦ In the mist of temptation, I shall stand steadfast, un-movable, and continually abound in the strength of the Lord. *I Corinthians 15:58*

♦ I shall keep my body under, and bring it in subjec-tion to my spirit. *I Corinthians 9:27*

♦ I am an overcomer. I overcome all evil, temptations, addictions, and strongholds through the power of Jesus Christ. Because greater is Jesus Christ who lives, abides, and dwells within me, than the enemy that is in the world. *I John 4:4*

♦ I am born of God; therefore, I overcome the world. For I am a victorious overcomer through my faith and strength in Christ Jesus. *I John 5:4*

♦ I am sober (prayerful and watchful) in the Lord, be-cause I know that my adversary, the devil, is as a roaring lion seeking whom he may devour. But he shall not de-vour me. *I Peter 5:8*

◆ Through the wisdom and strength of God, I abstain from all temptations and appearances of evil. *I Thessalonians 5:22*

◆ When I become weak, through Christ, I am made strong. *II Corinthians 12:10*

◆ God's grace is sufficient for me. For when I am weak in myself, I am strengthened in Him. *II Corinthians 12:9*

◆ The Spirit of the Lord is upon me and in me. And where the spirit of the Lord is, there is strength and liberty. *II Corinthians 3:17*

◆ I am in Christ; I am therefore a new person in Him. My old life of sin, perversion, abominations, and ungodly addictions have all passed away. And now, all things have become new. I no longer have the nature of sin and the world. I now have a new nature—the nature of Christ. *II Corinthians 5:17*

◆ The Lord knows how to deliver me out of every temptation and stronghold. *II Peter 2:9*

◆ I know in whom I have believed: For I am fully persuaded that He is well able to keep me from sin, and deliver me from every temptation and stronghold. *II Timothy 1:12*

◆ I am a vessel of honor unto the Lord. I have been purged by the Holy Spirit, and I am sanctified and meet (available) for the Lord's use, and prepared to do His good work. *II Timothy 2:21*

◆ The Lord shall deliver me from every evil work and temptation of the enemy, and He shall preserve me unto His heavenly Kingdom. *II Timothy 4:18*

♦ I walk victoriously unto the Lord, desiring to please Him at all times. His Spirit produces good fruit in my life, and I continually grow in the knowledge of God, and in the strength of His Word. *Colossians 1:10*

♦ God has delivered me from every power and stronghold of darkness, and He has translated me to the power and influence of His Son, Jesus Christ. *Colossians 1:13*

♦ I discipline the members of my body through the Word of God. *Colossians 3:5*

♦ My mind, heart, and my life are renewed day by day through the Word of God. *Ephesians 4:23*

♦ I have put on the new man. For I have been born of God, and created in His image and in His righteousness to live a life that is holy and pleasing unto Him. *Ephesians 4:24*

♦ I walk in the spirit, and I will therefore give no place to the devil in my life. *Ephesians 4:27*

♦ I put on the whole armor on God each and every day. And as I put on my armor, I am able to stand against all the temptations, tricks, and seductions of the devil. *Ephesians 6:11*

♦ I stand strong in the Lord by having my mind wrapped up in His Word. I wear the breastplate of His power and righteousness, and my feet are covered with His anointing and His peace. *Ephesians 6:14-15*

♦ Above all things, I take the shield of faith. And with it, I am able to overcome all the fiery darts of temptations and strongholds of the enemy. *Ephesians 6:16*

♦ I have been crucified with Christ; nevertheless I live. Yet it is not I that live, but Jesus Christ who lives in me.

And the life that I now live in the flesh, I am able to live it victoriously by the power, faith, and strength of the Son of God, who loves me, and gave His life for me. *Galatians 2:20*

♦ I stand strong and unmovable in my place of victory and liberty by which Christ has made me free, and I am watchful, to not allow myself to become entangled with yokes of bondage. *Galatians 5:1*

♦ I walk and live under the power and influence of the Holy Ghost. Therefore, I do not give in to, nor do I fulfill the lusts or temptations of the flesh. *Galatians 5:16*

♦ I am born of God through Christ Jesus, and I have crucified the lusts and the affections of my flesh. *Galatians 5:24*

♦ The Word of God is quick, powerful, and sharper than any two-edged sword, piercing even to the dividing asunder of the soul and spirit. And as I confess the Word of God over my life, it cuts away all ungodly desires, addictions, and habits from my mind, my heart, and my soul. *Hebrews 4:12*

♦ I lay aside every weight (every obstacle and temptation) that causes me to sin, and I am therefore able to run victoriously in Christ, the race that is set before me. *Hebrews 12:1*

♦ Through Christ Jesus I am able to endure and overcome all temptations. *James 1:12*

♦ I am victorious in Christ over all temptations and strongholds, because I am a doer of the Word of God, and not just a hearer only. *James 1:22*

♦ Since Christ has set me free from the bondage of sin

and temptation, I am therefore free indeed. *John 8:36*

♦ The Lord is able to keep me from falling to any temptation, sin, or stronghold, and to present me faultless before the presence of His glory with exceeding joy. *Jude 1:24*

♦ Jesus Christ has given me the power and authority to overcome all the powers, temptations, and seductions of the enemy. *Luke 9:1*

♦ Jesus Christ has prayed for me, and He is continually on the right hand of the Father interceding for me so that my faith and strength will not fail. *Luke 22:32*

♦ When I am tempted of the devil, I will not take (receive) any of his unrighteous, immoral, or ungodly thoughts. Instead, I will do like Jesus, and rebuke every one of the devils thoughts with the Word of God. *Matthew 6:25, Matthew 4:2-11, James 4:7*

♦ I am watchful and prayerful at all times; therefore, I shall not give *in* to temptation. For I know that my spirit is strong and willing to obey God, but my flesh (at times) becomes weak. *Matthew 26:41*

♦ The Lord upholds me. He keeps me from falling into the snare of temptation, and He delivers me from evil, and from the evil one. *Matthew 6:13*

♦ The joy of the Lord is my strength, and I have the strength of the Lord to overcome sin, strongholds, and addictions. *Nehemiah 8:10*

♦ I am disciplined in the Word of God to hide His Word deep within my heart continually; therefore, I shall not disobey God or sin against His Word. *Psalms 119:11*

◆ The Lord restores my soul and strength, and He leads me in the path of His righteousness for His name-sake. *Psalms 23:3*

◆ I present my body unto the Lord as a living sacrifice—one that is holy and acceptable unto Him. For this is my reasonable service. *Romans 12:1*

◆ I am not conformed to the image, thoughts, or lifestyle of the world. Instead, I am transformed unto the Lord Jesus Christ as I renew my mind in the Word of God day by day. Therefore, I am able to please Him and do those things that are good, acceptable, and perfect in His sight. *Romans 12:2*

◆ I cast off every work of darkness by the power of the Holy Ghost, and I put on the armor of light. *Romans 13:12*

◆ I put on and keep on the Lord Jesus Christ, and I make no provisions for my flesh. *Romans 13:14*

◆ My old nature has been crucified with Christ; therefore, I do not serve sin. *Romans 6:6*

◆ There is no condemnation in me, because I am in Christ Jesus, and I do not walk or live under the influence or control of the flesh, but rather, under the control and influence of the Spirit. *Romans 8:1*

◆ I am more than a conqueror over all sin and temptations because of Jesus Christ who loves me. *Romans 8:37*

Confessions For Power Over Lust and Sexual Sins

♦ There is no temptation that can come upon me, but those that have come upon others. But God is faithful, who will not allow me to be tempted above that which I am able to stand. And with every temptation that comes upon me, He will strengthen me, empower me, and enable me to overcome and escape the temptation. *I Corinthians 10:13*

♦ I shall keep my body under, and bring it in subjection to my spirit. *I Corinthians 9:27*

♦ I am an overcomer. And through the strength and power of Christ Jesus, I have the power to overcome the lust of the world (the lust of the eyes, lust of the flesh, and the pride of life). For these things are not of God, but of the world. *I John 2:16*

♦ I am an overcomer. I overcome all evil, temptations, and sins through the power of Jesus Christ. Because greater is Jesus Christ who lives, abides, and dwells within me, than the enemy that is in the world. *I John 4:4*

♦ It is through the Word of God and the power of the Holy Ghost that I walk sober in the Lord at all times—keeping my mind girded (wrapped up) in Christ. *I Peter 1:13*

♦ The Lord keeps me, and gives me the power to abstain from fleshly lusts which war against my soul. *I Peter 2:11*

♦ I am watchful, sober, and vigilant against the attacks of the devil, because I know that he is like a roaring lion seeking whom he may devour, but he shall not devour me. *I Peter 5:8*

♦ The Lord keeps me and helps me to abstain from all appearances of evil. *I Thessalonians 5:22*

♦ By the authority of Christ Jesus, I cast down every imagination of lust in my mind and in my heart. I also cast down every high spirit of seduction, lust, and lasciviousness that exalts itself against the knowledge of God. And with the Word of God, I bring into captivity every impure, unclean, ungodly, and immoral thought to the obedience of Christ. *II Corinthians 10:5*

♦ I am prayerful and watchful in the Holy Ghost; therefore, Satan shall not get an advantage over me with lust, because I am not ignorant to His devices. *II Corinthians 2:11*

♦ I have been born-again of the Spirit of God. Therefore, I am a new creature in Christ Jesus. The old (sinful, lustful, and lascivious) ways of my life have all passed away. And now, all things in my life have become new. I no longer have a nature of lust and sin. I now have a new nature—the nature of God through Christ Jesus. *II Corinthians 5:17*

♦ God is my strength and power over all forms and manners of lust, and He makes my way straight before Him. *II Samuel 22:33*

♦ I am confident in whom I believe (the Lord, Jesus Christ). And I am fully persuaded, that He is well able to keep me from any manner of lust and sin that the enemy brings against me. *II Timothy 1:12*

♦ Through the power and wisdom of God, I flee youthful lusts, and I follow after righteousness, faith, love, and peace—calling upon the name of the Lord out of a pure heart. *II Timothy 2:22*

♦ I have put off the old man, (the old life of sin and lust), and I have put on the new man, which is created in Christ Jesus. *Ephesians 4:22*

♦ God renews my mind and my strength in His spirit day by day. *Ephesians 4:23*

♦ I am watchful and diligent to stand guard over my soul with the Word of God; for I will not give any place to the devil in my life. *Ephesians 4:27*

♦ I am strong in the Lord and in the power of His might. I put on and I keep on the whole armor of God; therefore, I am well able to stand against all the snares, temptations, tricks, and deceptions of the devil. *Ephesians 10:6-11*

♦ I have been crucified with Christ; nevertheless I live. Yet it's not I that live, but Christ Jesus who lives within me. And the life that I now live in the flesh, I live it by the faith, power, and strength of the Son of God, who loves me, and gave Himself for me. *Galatians 2:20*

♦ I stand firm and strong in the liberty by which Christ Jesus has made me free from the power of lust and sin; and I will not allow myself to become entangled with lustful yokes of bondage. *Galatians 5:1*

♦ I am full of the Holy Ghost, and I walk continually in the spirit; therefore, I shall not fulfill the lusts of the flesh. *Galatians 5:16*

♦ I am born of God through Christ Jesus, and I have

crucified the lusts and affections of the flesh. *Galatians 5:24*

♦ The Word of God is quick, powerful, and sharper than any two-edged sword, piercing even to the dividing asunder of the soul and spirit. And as I confess the Word of God over my life, it cuts away all ungodly desires, addictions, and habits from my mind, my heart, and my soul. *Hebrews 4:12*

♦ It is through the power of the Holy Ghost that I am able to lay down every weight and sin of lust that tries to hold me back. And I run, with patience, the race that is set before me. *Hebrews 12:1*

♦ I am submitted unto God. I am also submitted to the Word of God and the Spirit of God. Therefore, I have the power (through Christ) to resist the devil, and He flees from me. *James 4:7*

♦ When I am tempted of the devil, I will not take (receive) any of his unrighteous, immoral, or ungodly thoughts. Instead, I will do like Jesus, and rebuke every one of the devils thoughts with the Word of God. *Matthew 6:25, Matthew 4:2-11, James 4:7*

♦ I keep watch, and I pray at all times. Therefore, I shall not enter or fall to temptation. I watch and pray because I understand that my spirit is willing to obey God and His Word, but my flesh (at times) becomes weak. *Matthew 26:41*

♦ The Lord keeps me from falling to overwhelming temptations, and He delivers me from all evil and traps of the devil. *Matthew 6:13*

♦ I will not allow my mind to become conformed to the lust, sin, and lasciviousness of this world. Instead, I will continually transform and renew my mind to the mind and image of Christ, as I pray and confess the Word of God. *Romans 12:2*

♦ I am well able (through the power of the Holy Ghost) to resist all sin and sexual temptation. For I can do all things through Christ who strengthens me. *Philippians 4:13*

♦ I will not allow Satan to manipulate, control, or occupy my mind. I will keep my mind upon things that are true, honest, just, pure, lovely, things that are of a good report, things of virtue, and things that give God praise. *Philippians 4:8*

♦ The Lord strengthens me and keeps me from being drawn to the seduction and temptations of the strange (luring or enticing) woman/man. *Proverbs 2:16*

♦ I keep guard over my heart with all diligence by prayer and the confession of the Word of God. For out of it (my heart) are the issues of life. *Proverbs 4:23*

♦ I will not (willfully) set any wicked thing before my eyes. I am disciplined in the Holy Ghost not to watch any movies, television programs, or anything else that would lead me to sin or lust. *Psalms 101:3*

♦ I present my body and my mind as a living sacrifice that is holy and acceptable unto the Lord. For this is my reasonable service unto Him. *Romans 12:1*

♦ I have put on the Lord Jesus Christ, and I will not give any allowances to my flesh to fulfill the lusts of the flesh in any way. *Romans 13:14*

♦ All the members and parts of my body belong to the Lord. And, I shall not yield any of the members of my body as instruments of unrighteous unto sin. Instead, I choose to yield the members of my body unto the Lord as instruments of righteousness unto Him. *Romans 6:13*

♦ Sin and lust has no power over me; neither do they have any dominion over me. For I am not under the law (control of the flesh), but under the grace of God (His control). *Romans 6:14*

♦ My body is the temple of the Holy Ghost. Therefore, I shall not yield my body to lust or sin in any manner. *Romans 6:16*

♦ My old man has been crucified with Christ. Therefore, lust and sin are destroyed in my life. For I live unto righteousness, and not unto sin. *Romans 6:6*

♦ There is now no condemnation in my life, because I choose not to walk after the lusts of flesh, but rather, after the Spirit of God. *Romans 8:1*

♦ I am victorious, and more than a conqueror over lust and sin in my life, by the power of the Holy Ghost. *Romans 8:37*

♦ The Lord strengthens me, and He empowers me to overcome lust, lasciviousness, and sexual sins and temptation—not by my own might, nor by my own power, but by the strength and power of the Lord of hosts. *Zechariah 4:6*

Confessions of God's Forgiveness—When You Have Sinned

♦ As I honestly and sincerely confess my sins before the Lord, He is faithful and merciful unto me to forgive me of my sins. And with the blood of Jesus Christ, He cleanses me from all of my unrighteousness. *I John 1:9*

♦ I do not walk in sin, but in the righteousness of Jesus Christ. But, if I happen to fall into sin, I have an advocate with the Father through Jesus Christ, His Son. *I John 2:1*

♦ God has made Christ Jesus to be sin for me—who knew no sin, that I would be made the righteousness of God through Christ Jesus. *II Corinthians 5:21*

♦ As a child of God, the Lord is merciful unto me. And as I confess my sins, He is merciful to forgive me of my unrighteousness, and not to remember my sins anymore. *Hebrews 8:12*

♦ When I repent (from my heart), the Lord blots out my transgressions and sins for His own namesake, and He does not charge them against me. *Isaiah 43:25*

♦ God sent His own Son into the world, not to condemn the world, but so that those in the world would have an opportunity to receive salvation (through His Son, Jesus Christ). Therefore, I refuse to walk in condemnation, because God has saved and forgiven me, and He has released me from the condemnation of sin. *John 3:17*

♦ I forgive and release others who have wronged,

sinned, and trespassed against me. And as I have forgiven them, the Lord is faithful to also forgive me of my sins, trespasses, and iniquities. *Luke 11:4*

♦ When I have committed transgressions against the Lord (and I repent of them and turn to Him), it is His glory to forgive me of my transgressions. *Proverbs 19:11*

♦ No matter how many times I fall, the Lord is full of grace and mercy to forgive me, and raise me up again. *Proverbs 24:16*

♦ Because of the Lord Jesus Christ, God does not deal with me according to my sins; neither does He reward me according to my iniquities. But His mercy shines bright upon me. *Psalms 103:10*

♦ When I confess my sins unto the Lord, He removes them from me as far as the east is from the west. *Psalms 103:12*

♦ I will bless the Lord from the depths of my soul. And with all that is within me, I will bless His holy name. For I am careful not to forget any of His benefits. For the Lord forgives all of my iniquities and my transgressions. *Psalms 103:2-3*

♦ I am blessed of the Lord because He has forgiven my transgressions, and covered my sins. *Psalms 32:1*

♦ I have acknowledged my sins unto the Lord, and I have not hidden my iniquities from Him; therefore, He has forgiven me. *Psalms 32:5*

♦ Because I have had a broken spirit (concerning my sins), and a contrite (repentive and sorrowful) heart, the Lord has forgiven my transgressions, and He has drawn me near to Him again. *Psalms 34:18*

♦ Though I have fallen, I have not been utterly cast down. For the Lord upholds me with His hand. *Psalms 37:24*

♦ When I cried out to the Lord concerning my sins, He heard my cry. He brought me up out of a horrible pit of sin and condemnation. He has forgiven me, set my feet upon a rock, and reestablished me. *Psalms 40:1-2*

♦ When I repent and cry unto the Lord, He creates a clean heart within me, and renews me with a right spirit. *Psalms 51:10*

♦ The Lord restores unto me the joy of His salvation, and He upholds me with His spirit of forgiveness. *Psalms 51:12*

Confessions to Give You Strength in the Lord

♦ I am born of God. I have the strength to overcome the evil one and all manners of sin and temptation. For greater is He (Jesus Christ) who strengthens me and dwells within me, than the enemy that is in the world. *1 John 4:4*

♦ The God of all grace establishes me, strengthens me, and settles me in Christ Jesus, our Lord. *I Peter 5:10*

♦ The Lord renews my faith, and He strengthens me in my inner man day by day. *II Corinthians 4:16*

♦ I grow daily in the grace of God, and in the knowledge, understanding, and faith of Jesus Christ. *II Peter 3:18*

♦ The Lord keeps the fire of the Holy Ghost stirred up within me. *II Peter 1:6*

♦ Because the Holy Ghost has come upon me, I have received the power, anointing, and the fire of God to be an effective witness upon my job, my home, and everywhere I go. *Acts 1:8*

♦ I am strengthened with the might of God according to the glorious power of the Lord. *Colossians 1:11*

♦ I am a man/woman of faith. I am grounded and settled in my faith, and I shall not be moved away from the hope of the gospel which I have heard. *Colossians 1:23*

♦ I am filled with the power and strength of God, and with the knowledge of His will in all wisdom and spiritual understanding. *Colossians 1:9*

♦ I am well-rooted and built up in Christ Jesus, and I am established in the faith of Christ. *Colossians 2:7*

♦ According to the riches and glory of God, the Lord has strengthened me with His might by His Spirit. *Ephesians 3:16*

♦ I am continually renewed in the spirit of my mind by the Holy Ghost. *Ephesians 4:23*

♦ I am strong in the Lord and in the power and strength of His might. *Ephesians 6:10*

♦ The Lord makes me mature in the spirit so that I may do His will. He works in and through me, so that I may please Him, and bring pleasure to His sight through Jesus Christ. *Hebrews 13:21*

♦ When I am weak or faint in my faith or my walk with Christ, the Lord empowers me, and He increases my strength. *Isaiah 40:29*

♦ I will not fear or be dismayed, because the Lord is with me. He strengthens me, helps me, encourages me, and upholds me with the right hand of His righteousness. *Isaiah 41:10*

♦ The Lord strengthens me, and He makes me as stable as a tree that is planted by the waters, that spreads out its root in the river. *Jeremiah 17:8*

♦ I build myself up (daily) with strength in my spirit-man as I pray in the Holy Ghost. *Jude 1:20*

♦ As I speak and confess the Word of God, He renews my strength every morning. Great is the faithfulness of the

Lord. *Lamentations 3:23*

♦ It is my joy in the Lord that gives me strength. For the joy of the Lord is my strength. *Nehemiah 8:10*

♦ I grow continually in the Lord, coming to know Him more and more each day. I grow in knowing Him in the power of His resurrection (the demonstration of miracles, signs and wonders), and in the fellowship of His sufferings (my service, love, and sacrifice unto Him). *Philippians 3:10*

♦ I have the power of the Holy Ghost within me. Therefore, I can do all things through Christ who strengthens me. *Philippians 4:13*

♦ Whenever I cry unto the Lord for strength, He empowers me with His strength in my soul. *Psalms 138:3*

♦ It is the Lord who girds and establishes me with strength, and He makes my way right, perfect, and mature in Him. *Psalms 18:32*

♦ The Lord restores the strength of my soul, and He leads me in His path of righteous for His namesake. *Psalms 23:3*

♦ Whenever I need strength, I call upon the Lord and wait upon Him, and He renews the strength of my heart. *Psalms 27:14*

♦ The Lord restores and renews my salvation, and He upholds me with His strong spirit. *Psalms 51:12*

♦ As I seek the Lord each day, He anoints me with the fresh oil of His presence. *Psalms 92:10*

Confessions
of Peace and Comfort

♦ God has not given me a spirit of fear or unrest, but He has given unto me a spirit of power, and of love, and a sound and peaceful mind. *2 Timothy 1:7*

♦ I abide in the peace of God, and I allow His peace to rule my heart each and every day. *Colossians 3:15*

♦ The Lord has ordained peace for my life, and He has established all of my works in Him. *Isaiah 26:12*

♦ The Lord keeps me continually in His perfect peace, because I keep my heart and mind stayed and fastened upon Him. *Isaiah 26:3*

♦ Because I abide in the Lord, I shall continually dwell in peaceable habitations, and in quiet resting places all the days of my life. *Isaiah 32:18*

♦ God has given unto me His peace. He has not given to me the peace of the world, but rather, the peace of God. Therefore, my heart shall not be troubled, and neither shall I be afraid. *John 14:27*

♦ As Jesus rebuked the wind and raging sea, and commanded them to be at peace, He has also given me the authority to decree peace upon the storms of my life. Therefore, I decree and declare, "Peace, be still," to every disturbance and storm in my life. *Mark 4:39*

♦ The Lord continually lifts up His countenance upon me, and He gives me His peace. *Numbers 6:26*

♦ The peace of God that passes all of man's understanding shall keep my heart and mind established in Christ Jesus. *Philippians 4:7*

♦ Because I love and dwell in the Word of God, I have great peace upon my life and upon my heart; therefore, I shall not allow anything to worry or trouble me. *Psalms 119:165*

♦ Even in the midst of the storm, the Lord causes me to lie down in quiet, green pastures, and He leads me beside peaceful, still waters. *Psalms 23:2*

♦ I am in the Kingdom of God; therefore, I have the righteousness of God, the peace of God, and the joy of the Holy Ghost. *Romans 14:17*

♦ My heart follows after things that produce peace, and things that bring edification. *Romans 14:19*

♦ The God of hope fills me with all joy and peace, and He blesses me to abide in hope through the power of the Holy Ghost. *Romans 15:13*

♦ I am justified by faith, and I have the peace of God through our Lord, Jesus Christ. Romans 5:1

♦ God is not the author of confusion, but rather, the author of peace and joy in my heart and my life. *1 Corinthians 14:33*

♦ I keep my mind upon things that are true, honest, just, pure, lovely, things that are of a good report, and things that have virtue and praise. *Philippians 4:8*

Confessions for When You Need Encouragement

♦ As David was in distress and discouragement because of His circumstances, He encouraged himself in the Lord. I shall therefore likewise encourage myself in the Lord. *I Samuel 30:6*

♦ The Lord is the God of all comfort. He comforts me in times of tribulation and trouble, and He also comforts me in times of discouragement and despair. *II Corinthians 1:3-4*

♦ Where the Spirit of the Lord is, there is strength and liberty. *II Corinthians 3:17*

♦ As I wait upon the Lord (through prayer, confession, worship, and the fellowship in His Word), He renews my strength. He causes me to rise up (from the place of despair) like the wings of an eagle. Through His strength and encouragement, He enables me to go forward each day, and not become weary or discouraged. He also causes me to walk by faith, and not give in or give up. *Isaiah 40:31*

♦ I will not walk in fear or discouragement, because the Lord is with me. He shall be my strength; He shall help me, and He shall uphold me with the right hand of His strength and His righteousness. *Isaiah 41:10*

♦ When the spirit of heaviness (discouragement, despair or depression) comes upon me, I will put on the garment of praise. I will bless the Lord and give worship and praise unto Him. And, as I do so, the Lord shall give me strength. *Isaiah 61:3*

♦ When I am discouraged and heavily burdened with cares, concerns, and trouble in my life, I will give them unto the Lord—who gives me rest. I will exchange my yoke of heaviness for His yoke of peace, comfort, and rest unto my soul. For the yoke of the Lord is easy, and His burden is light. *Matthew 11:28-29*

♦ In times of sorrow, sadness, and discouragement, the Lord fills me with His joy. For the joy of the Lord is my strength. *Nehemiah 8:10*

♦ In times of sadness and despair, the Lord blesses me and strengthens me. He causes His face and presence to shine upon me; He lifts up my countenance, and gives me His peace. *Numbers 6:24-26*

♦ When my spirit is broken, the Lord shall mend my heart. He shall give me a merry heart, which heals my spirit like medicine. *Proverbs 17:22*

♦ When my heart is broken and discouraged, the Lord heals my heart and binds up my wounds. *Psalms 147:3*

♦ In my times of affliction, I will dwell in the presence of the Lord. For in the presence of the Lord is the fullness of joy, and at His right hand there are pleasures forevermore. *Psalms 16:11*

♦ I will always set the Lord before me. And because He goes before me, I shall not be moved. *Psalms 16:8*

♦ Whenever I am down or discouraged, the Lord restores my soul, and He leads me in His path of righteousness for His namesake. *Psalms 23:3*

♦ In times of discouragement, I shall wait upon the Lord with prayer, confession, and worship. And as I wait continually upon Him, He shall strengthen my heart.

Psalms 27:14

♦ The Lord is my protection. He is my shield and my glory. And in times of distress or discouragement, He is the lifter of my head. *Psalms 3:3*

♦ In times of mourning and sorrow, the Lord girds me with His gladness, and turns my mourning and sorrow into joy, laughter, and dancing. *Psalms 30:11*

♦ Times of sadness and weeping will only endure for a night for me. But because the Lord is with me, my joy shall come soon in the morning. *Psalms 30:5*

♦ My hope is in the Lord; therefore, I shall be of good courage, because He strengthens my heart. *Psalms 31:24*

♦ In times of trouble and affliction, the Lord brings me up, and out of the miry clay (of sadness, gloom, and sorrow), and He sets my feet upon a rock, and reestablishes my direction. *Psalms 40:2*

♦ Whenever I am down or discouraged, the Lord gives me a new song. As I worship Him and give Him praise, He gives me joy and peace. And because of the joy and peace of the Lord upon me (even through times of trouble and tribulation), many shall see me, and be drawn to put their trust in the Lord. *Psalms 40:3*

♦ I shall not allow my soul to stay in discouragement, because my hope is in God. For I will praise the Lord, who heals my countenance and restores my joy. *Psalms 43:5*

♦ I shall cast my burdens and afflictions upon the Lord in times of sorrow. For He shall sustain me with His peace, comfort, and joy, and He shall not allow me to be moved. *Psalms 55:22*

♦ There are times when I become discouraged and fainthearted, but God is the strength of my heart and my portion forever. *Psalms 73:26*

Confessions for When You Have Been Persecuted

♦ I shall not need to fight this battle alone. I will set myself and stand still, and see the salvation and deliverance of the Lord. *2 Chronicles 20:17*

♦ The Lord delivers me from those who come against me. *Daniel 6:16*

♦ The Lord contends (fight on my behalf) with every person, force, or spirit that comes against me. *Isaiah 49:25*

♦ No weapon that is formed against me—spiritually, physically, or by any other means, shall be able to prosper against me. And every word that is spoken against me shall fall to the ground. For this is my heritage as a servant of the Lord. *Isaiah 54:17*

♦ When people come against me and persecute me, and they say all manners of things against me falsely, I shall count myself blessed of the Lord. For great is my reward in heaven. *Matthew 5:11-12*

♦ The Lord has commanded me to forgive and pray for those who persecute and trespass against me. Therefore, I forgive those who have persecuted me. *Matthew 6:12-15*

♦ Many have persecuted me without a cause, but my heart stands still, firm, and confident in the Word of God, and in His deliverance. *Psalms 119:161*

♦ The Lord is faithful to His Word: When I am persecuted wrongly, it is the Lord who helps and delivers me.

Psalms 119:86

♦ When I am persecuted, the Lord delivers me from those who are against me, and from those that persecute me. *Psalms 31:15*

♦ I shall stand still and know that the Lord (He) is God, and He shall be exalted. For He is the one who shall deliver me. *Psalms 46:10*

♦ As I put my trust in the Lord, He saves and delivers me from those that persecute me. *Psalms 7:1*

♦ Because I have placed my love upon the Lord, He shall deliver me; He shall set me up in His secret place, because I have intimately known His name. *Psalms 91:14*

♦ Since God is for me, then no person, power, or force is strong enough or able to come against me and succeed in any way. *Romans 8:31*

♦ I shall not allow persecution or anything else to separate me from the love of God. *Romans 8:35*

♦ I will lift up mine eyes to the Lord—for He is the source of my help. My help comes only from Him. And, as I turn to Him, He hides me in His secret place, and delivers me from those who are against me. *Psalms 121:2, Psalms 143:9*

Confessions
For Your Church and Pastor

♦ The Lord has established _____ as a lighthouse for the city of _____ and the nation. *Matthew 5:14*

♦ People are standing in line to get into this church to hear the Word of God. They are drawn by the Spirit of God form the north, south, east, and west to every service, and every seat is filled in every service that we have. *Acts 2:47, Isaiah 43:6, Malachi 3:10*

♦ Our pastor is called and appointed by God as the pastor and leader of our church. God has anointed him with knowledge, wisdom, and understanding to teach and preach the Word of God with clarity and understanding. *Luke 4:18, Isaiah 11:2, Jeremiah 3:15*

♦ Miracles, signs, and wonders take place in every one of our services. People are saved, set free, restored unto the Lord, and delivered from every stronghold and bondage of the enemy in every service. *Mark 16:20, Psalms 23:3*

♦ We are a church of unity, and there is no division among us. We are all on one accord. We are all of the same mind and same spirit. *Psalms 133:1, 1 Corinthians 1:10, Ephesians 4:3*

♦ We grow in love as a church, and we also grow in the grace and knowledge of Jesus Christ and the Word of God. *2 Peter 3:18*

♦ Every member of our church is assembled in their proper place (of service), and they do not forsake the assembly when it is time to come together. *Hebrews 10:25*

♦ Every member of our church is filled with the vision that God has given to us. And, they support the vision with their commitment, love, and financial support. *Habakkuk 2:2-3, Proverbs 29:18*

♦ Every member of our church studies the Word of God, and they are faithful hearers and doers of the Word of God; therefore, they are rooted, grounded, and established in the faith, and are not moved away by any temptation or doctrine. *2 Timothy 2:15, James 1:22, Colossians 1:23*

♦ Every need in this ministry, and in the lives of our members is met. All of our property, buildings, and assets are paid off in full, and we owe nothing to anyone but love. Every member of this church is covered under the canopy of God's protection, and they are healed, healthy, blessed and prosperous. *Philippians 4:19, Romans 3:8, Psalms 91:1, 3 John 1:2*

♦ No weapon that is formed against our church, pastor, or any members of our church can prosper against us. For we are anointed by God, and the gates of hell cannot prevail against us. *Isaiah 54:17, Matthew 16:18*

♦ We are victorious, and more than conquerors through Christ who has ordained and established us. And, we go forth continually to declare our victory through the power and authority of God in Christ Jesus. *Romans 8:37*

Confession
For Our Nation

♦ As I pray and confess the Word of God over America, and our leaders, the Lord shall bless us to live quiet and peaceable lives in all godliness and honesty. *1 Timothy 2:1-2*

♦ Because the people of God (in America) humble themselves and pray, the Lord hears our prayers, forgives our sins, and heals our land. *2 Chronicles 7:14*

♦ America is a great nation. For we are blessed by the Lord. *Deuteronomy 4:6*

♦ I am an intercessor. I avail myself to I make up the hedge and stand in the gap as I pray and confess God's Word over America. Therefore, the Lord will not allow destruction to come upon us. *Ezekiel 22:30*

♦ No weapon that is formed against America (spiritually or physically) shall be able to prosper against us. I confess the Word of God therefore that no weapon of terrorism, sabotage, nor any other weapon of destruction shall be able to prosper against this nation, or the people of this nation. *Isaiah 54:17*

♦ I decree that Satan's will of stealing, killing and destruction is prohibited from operating in our nation. And only the will of God, which is to give life unto our nation, and life more abundantly (God's blessings of prosperity, provisions and protection) shall be upon us. *Matthew 6:10*

♦ The Lord's hand is upon our nation, and He delivers us from all evil and destruction. *Matthew 6:13*

◆ Because America puts it's trust in the Lord, the Lord shows us His marvelous kindness, and defends us from the wicked that rise up against us. *Psalms 17:7-9*

◆ America is blessed because the Lord is still the God of our nation. *Psalms 33:12*

◆ Because the people of God in America still love, respect, and reverence the Lord, His mercy is still upon us. *Psalms 103:17*

◆ God is with us (as a nation); therefore, there is no nation, group of people, power, or force that can stand or prosper against us. *Romans 8:31*

New and Exciting

"The Weapons of Our Warfare, Volume III"

The Weapons of Our
WARFARE
Volume III

The Keys to the Kingdom

Confessing the Word of God with Authority

By Kenneth Scott

We now have two exciting cassette series. You already know about the Weapons of Our Warfare Prayers from volumes 1 & 2 on cassette tape. Well, get ready! We now have *"The Weapons of Our Warfare, Volume 3 (Confessions)"* on cassette tape and CD as well.

Most of you already know that if we are going to obtain and maintain victory in our lives, that we must be disciplined to pray the Word of God. But God not only commands us to pray His Word, but to also keep our minds *"transformed and renewed"* by (continually) speaking, or rather, confessing His Word.

Pastor Scott has spent over three years researching hundreds of scriptures that are focused to "strike the mark" for just about every major area in your life. He has taken each scripture and arranged them in   personalized confession form, making it easy for you to flow in the spirit of "*Confession Warfare*" with each one.

Pastor Scott will lead you into each confession, allowing space for you to follow and confess each scripture confession after him. You can confess the Word of God along with Pastor Scott while you are driving your car going to and from work, while cleaning your home, or while just simply meditating on the Word of God.

Pastor Scott uses this series daily himself, and highly recommends this series for every Christian that is determined to keep their mind on Christ, walk in victory, and obtain, as well as maintain the promises of God.

Request your copy today by calling our order line at (205) 853-9509, or Visit our website at www.spiritualwarfare.cc

Other Books and Materials
By Kenneth Scott

The Weapons Of Our Warfare, Volume 1

This is a handbook of scriptural based prayers for just about every need in your life. There are prayers for your home, marriage, family and many personal issues that we face in our lives each day. If you desire to be developed in prayer, then this is a must book for you.

The Weapons Of Our Warfare, Volume 2

It is a sequel of volume I, and brings the prayer warrior into the ministry of intercession. It has prayers for your church, pastor, city, our nation, and many other issues in which we should pray for. If you desire to be developed as an intercessor, then this book is for you.

The Weapons Of Our Warfare, Volume 4
—Prayers for Teens and Young Adults

Teenagers have different needs than adults. This is a prayer handbook that keeps the same fervency and fire as volume 1 & 2, but also addresses the needs of teens. This book is a "must" for your Teens.

The Weapons Of Our Warfare Volume 1 & 2
on Audio Cassette

Meditate on the anointed Word of God as it is prayed on audio cassette tapes. These tapes contain prayers from volume 1 & 2. There is also a healing tape with the healing prayer, along with over 70 healing scriptures. As You hear these prayers prayed, you can stand in the spirit of agreement and apply them in the spirit to your life, situations and circumstances as you ride in your car, or as you sit in your home. These tapes are a must for every Christian library.

The Weapons Of Our Warfare Volume 3 on Audio
Cassette and CD

This cassette tape series contains the same confessions that are in "The Weapons of Our Warfare, Volume III." Pastor Scott will lead you in confessions, allowing you to easily follow and quote them afterwards. Make confessions of the Word of God throughout your day as you sit in your home or drive in your car.

The Weapons Of Our Warfare, Spanish Edition
Coming in June 2003

When All Hell Breaks Loose
Most mature Christians can survive the casual trial here and there, but many of God's people fall during the storms of life. Get this book and learn how to prevail through the storm *"When all Hell Breaks Loose."*

Praying in Your Divine Authority
Many Christians are hindered and defeated by Satan simply because they do not know the dominion and authority they have in Christ. This book teaches the believer how to bind and loose Satan and demon spirits, and how to pray and walk in our divine authority. *Now Available*

Understanding The Lord's Prayer
Just about all of us have prayed "The Lord's Prayer," and even know The Lord's prayer by memory. But very few of us really understand the depths of what Jesus was truly teaching His disciples in this prayer outline. This book gives the believer a scripture by scripture breakdown of this prayer and gives illumination and insight on its understanding. *Coming May 2003*

Standing In The Gap
Coming in June 2003

Decreeing your Healing — Mini-booklet
This mini-booklet conveniently has the healing prayer, along with the full scriptures passage of over 70 healing scriptures. It is great to either have yourself in case you come under physical attack, or to share with others you have prayed for.

Cassette Taped Messages
We have inspiring, powerful and anointed cassette taped messages of Evangelist Scott. Visit us on the web to see a listing of available cassette tapes.

For other available materials,
visit us on the web at www.spiritualwarfare.cc.

Notes:

Notes

Notes

Notes

Notes